CUISINE
OF THE SUN

Roger Vergé, one of the most unusual of the great French chefs, was born in Commentry in 1930. He served his apprenticeship locally and in 1950 moved to Paris, first at the Tour d'Argent and then at the Hotel Plaza-Athénee. His love of the sun took him in 1953 to the kitchens of the most important hotels of North Africa, returning to France in 1961.

From 1961 to 1969 he directed the kitchen of the Club à Cavalière, one of the best restaurants in the South of France with two Michelin stars. Since 1969, helped by his wife Denise, he has managed his own restaurant, the Moulin de Mougins, which achieved its third star in 1974.

CUISINE OF THE SUN

Roger Vergé

Edited and adapted by
Caroline Conran

M

Ma Cuisine du Soleil
Les Recettes originales de Roger Vergé
© Editions Robert Laffont S.A., Paris 1978

This English translation and adaptation
© Macmillan London 1979

ISBN 0 333 31919 2

CUISINE OF THE SUN
first published 1979 by
MACMILLAN LONDON LTD
4 Little Essex Street London WC2R 3LF
and Basingstoke

First published in 1981 by
PAPERMAC
a division of Macmillan Publishers
Limited London and Basingstoke

Associated companies in Auckland, Dallas,
Delhi, Dublin, Hong Kong, Johannesburg, Lagos,
Manzini, Melbourne, Nairobi, New York,
Singapore, Tokyo, Washington and
Zaria

Translation by Caroline Conran and Caroline Hobhouse
Photographs by Didier Blanchat

Printed in Great Britain by
BUTLER & TANNER LTD
Frome and London

Contents

List of Illustrations

Colour Plates

Between pages 64 and 65

Sea-Bass Fillets with Lettuce Leaves, Red Mullet, Pierrot's Way and Escalopes of Salmon Marinated with Basil

Saddle of Rabbit Salad, Nage of Freshwater Crayfish Tails with Beurre Blanc, Medallions of Veal with Lemon and Fresh Fruit Sorbets

John Dory with Spring Vegetables

Between pages 192 and 193

Estouffade of Lamb Stew with Garlic Bread

Provençal Stuffed Vegetables

Mikado Salad and Harlequin Omelette

Lemon Tart, Orange Cream, Oeufs à la Neige with Peach Leaves and Pralines, and Winter Fruit Salad in Wine

Introduction
by
Caroline Conran

Roger Vergé, of all the master-chefs working in France today, is probably the one whose ideas are most accessible to home cooks. It is partly because his restaurant is in Provence and many of his dishes have the warm Provençal flavour so beloved of all good cooks. Partly, too, because he has never lost sight of the fact that cooking should be a pleasure – a celebration of wonderful ingredients, cooked in a simple and practical way that will not over-tax the cook and leave her (or him) too exhausted to enjoy the meal. Very few of his recipes follow the pattern that most top chefs prefer, of complex compositions based on the gruelling prepara-tions of the brigade de cuisine: pretty, last-minute bits of cheffery combining finely-sliced truffles, poached asparagus tips, sliced lobster and complicated sauces may appear in his restaurant but they do not find house-room in this book. He has concentrated much of his attention on the simple stuffed vegetables, oeufs au plat, anchoïade, fish soups, estouffades and pâtés of his own region, or on recipes prepared by or for his friends. There is, of course, a sprinkling of extravagant recipes too, because this is, after all, unmistakably haute cuisine. But even these recipes are undaunting because they are straightforward.

There is much to learn from Roger Vergé. There are, for example, at least three perfectly wonderful methods of cooking fish, which can be used over and over again with all sorts and varieties of fish. His ways of cooking duck are brilliant, and he solves the eternal problem of cooking kidneys without stewing them in their own juice.

Having explained away so many of the basic problems of cooking the main ingredients, Vergé adds to them his own flavours and in-novations. Pheasant is served with endives in cream (*page 190*), sea-bream with orange and lemon stewed in olive oil (*page 130*), the custard for oeufs à la neige is flavoured with peach leaves (*page 292*), red mullet are accompanied by little pieces of toast spread with a fennel purée (*page 134*), rabbit is served with a cream sauce flavoured with basil (*page 188*). Each recipe is a carefully planned experiment using a simple balance of flavours, each one of which is there for a reason (and not just for the sake of doing something new).

A great many of Roger Vergé's innovations, although simple, are surprising, but apart from his occasional excursions into the tropics, where he found his passion for old rum and the flavour of cooked coconut, his recipes do not generally require any particularly extraordinary ingredients.

Unfortunately, however, some of the things regarded as perfectly ordinary by those who do their shopping in the seductive atmosphere of the daily vegetable markets in Nice or Cannes, turn out to be near impossibilities for anybody else. Where, oh where can one obtain French beans the size of fork prongs, with their white flowers still attached? Or the round little aubergines and courgettes that Vergé finds so ideal for stuffing? Or the fresh white onions and interesting salad leaves such as roquette that he prefers for some dishes? One answer is, obviously, to grow them. Anybody who has access to a vegetable garden will find, next time they go to Paris, that a browse along the Quai Voltaire will take them past rows of plant and seed shops where they can spend a really happy afternoon buying all sorts of interesting vegetable seeds to try out at home. (You can also, of course, search the more enterprising seedsmen's catalogues and order seeds by post.) These obliging seeds nearly always find it perfectly possible to grow happily in any domesticated English soil, although since our summers are so unpredictable, it is best to plant aubergines and basil under a south-facing wall or better still in a greenhouse, or in pots on a sunny windowsill. Failing this counsel of perfection, use ordinary vegetables of as good a quality as you can find.

Apart from vegetables, there is one ingredient used in this book with what seems like inordinate extravagance – olive oil. For many people who live far away from olive groves, it has become a matter of habit to use other vegetable oils for cooking, and to keep the precious olive oil for salads. Do not make this mistake when using Vergé's recipes (unless he specifically suggests a different oil). They very much depend on the glorious fruity flavour of olives which permeates the food with a special character that is very important. In his own restaurant Vergé uses it liberally; he even serves his foie gras de canard with a spoonful of the very fruitiest olive oil, together with a few leaves from the inside of a Batavian endive and a very, very thinly sliced raw apple sprinkled with lemon juice. It is a surprisingly successful combination, giving freshness and digestibility to what can sometimes be an overpoweringly rich dish.

For, although he uses butter abundantly and cream fairly lavishly, he does agree with other upholders of the Nouvelle Cuisine that haute cuisine should generally be light and more healthy than it used to be. His stews and estouffades, for example, are free of fat and avoid heavy, floury indigestible sauces. And his ratatouille (*page 216*) is cooked only for a few minutes instead of the usual hour or two, an experiment worth trying if you like vegetables lightly cooked. Incidentally, this is one recipe that requires an enormous amount of hand work – peeling, chopping and slicing. But for several of the more complex dishes, a Magi-mix or robot-chef is a helpful gadget, and for the sorbets (*pages 250–258*) a sorbetière gives the ice a perfect fine texture and is well worth the out-lay. Vergé also uses, as do all French chefs, a wooden spatula for moving fragile food and folding delicate mixtures, a job which it does perform with less damage than a wooden spoon. This can be obtained from a specialist kitchenware shop, or a metal spatula with a wooden handle can be used instead.

In the pudding chapter there are recipes for unpretentious and re-strained puddings – light tarts, clafoutis (*page 290*) and wonder-fully easy fresh fruit sorbets (*pages 250–258*) which far outdo any fussy and complicated desserts. Particularly worth making is the pâte sablée made with ground almonds and rum. This pastry, care-fully made, rolled out and cooked in flat discs makes the base of several really fresh tarts, such as lemon or raspberry (*pages 280–284*), which are vastly lighter than the usual versions and very little trouble to make. This is typical of Vergé's style, he knows how to make things better without going into complications, and it is for this simplicity as well as for his deep knowledge and interesting ideas that serious cooks will want to keep using this book.

Measurements

Since the introduction of metric measurements in the kitchen in Britain and elsewhere, cookery-book writers have been faced with all sorts of headaches, as it is now necessary to give two different measurements at once.

In this book the usual business of converting pounds and ounces to grammes has been reversed, but the problems remain the same.

The difficulty lies in finding sensible equivalents – one ounce actually equals 28.350 grammes, for example. So to prevent situations where the reader is supposed to measure out 0·353 of an ounce (10 grammes), and so on, we have followed the usual practice of rounding the quantities up or down to the nearest number of ounces or pints.

However, even so, some measurements are distinctly fiddly, so we suggest taking the (eventually) inevitable plunge and obtaining metric scales and measuring jug – you can then use Roger Vergé's original measurements.

If this is impossible, use your own judgement as to whether it is important to be exact or not.

Conversion Tables

WEIGHT

1. Exact equivalents (to two places of decimals)

Metric	British
25 g	0·88 oz
100 g	3·53 oz
1 kg	2·20 lb
British	Metric
1 oz	28·35 g
8 oz	226·78 g
1 lb	0·45 kg (453·6 g)
1½ lb	0·68 kg (680·40 g)
2 lb	0·91 kg (907·2 g)

2. Approximate equivalents

Metric	British
25 g	1 oz
50 g	1¾–2 oz
75 g	2½ oz
100 g	3½ oz
200 g	7 oz
500 g (0·5 kg)	1 lb 2 oz (18 oz)
1000 g (1 kg)	2¼ lb (36 oz)

LIQUID MEASURES

1. Exact equivalents (to two places of decimals)

Metric	British
250 ml (0·25 litre)	0·44 pints
500 ml (0·50 litre)	0·88 pints
1 litre	1·76 pints
British	Metric
½ pint	0·28 litres
1 pint	0·57 litres

2. Approximate equivalents

Metric	British
150 ml	¼ pint
250 ml	scant half pint
300 ml	½ pint
500 ml (0·5 litre)	scant pint
750 ml	1¼ pints
1000 ml (1 litre)	1¾ pints
1·5 litres	2½ pints
2 litres	3½ pints

OVEN TEMPERATURES

Temperature equivalents for oven thermostat markings

Degrees Fahrenheit (°F)	Gas Regulo Mark	Degrees Centigrade (°C)
225	$\frac{1}{4}$	110
250	$\frac{1}{2}$	130
275	1	140
300	2	150
325	3	170
350	4	180
375	5	190
400	6	200
425	7	220
450	8	230
475	9	240
500	10	250

Foreword

For me, the pleasures of cooking are bound up with my memories of childhood. When I was five, my family and one or two friends gathered every Sunday and holiday in the great kitchen which also served us as dining-room and salon. The soul of that kitchen was embodied in a huge sombre green enamelled stove embellished with bright copper fittings, and the presiding fairy of the kitchen was my Tante Célestine. For my fifth birthday, she gave me a small wooden bench so that I could climb up, fascinated, to watch her cooking.

The memories of childhood are always so sweet. Over the years the outlines soften and lose their reality. The smallest landscapes become the Elysian fields, the cardboard horse becomes a charger and the first little local girlfriend takes on some of the qualities of the Madonna. However, one's first gastronomic experiences can be recalled with a wonderful clarity. I remember fresh as the day of creation carrots so fine and tender as to be almost transparent, the petits pois still clinging to their white flowers, the delicate, fragile lettuces, still pearled with dew, the little white onions no larger than tiny radishes, the appetising potatoes called 'ram's horns' which had only to be pressed in the hand to rub away the delicate skin.

My father was a blacksmith during the day, but in the evenings he tilled God's earth. And the tender bouquets of vegetables he brought in for my mother were so full of flavour and aroma that all that was needed was the addition of a few of the big rosy strips of pork fat which sizzled in the big cast-iron pot.

This was the 'cuisine heureuse', which consists of marrying natural products with one another, of finding simple harmonies and enhancing the flavour of each ingredient by contact with another with a complementary flavour.

The sweetness of onions, the 'green' taste of tomatoes, the acrid flavour of spinach, the sharpness of sorrel, the velvet texture of potatoes, the smoothness of the leek, the aroma of celery, of celeriac and of turnips, the honesty of garlic, the peppery bite of radishes – and the endless surprising flavours such as the delicate sweetness of fruits which can soften the bitterness of a vegetable and the exuberance of game – all these provide the infinitely subtle shades of flavour which give cooking its charm.

The 'cuisine heureuse' is the antithesis of cooking to impress – rich and pretentious. It is a light-hearted, healthy and natural way of cooking which combines the products of the earth like a bouquet of wild flowers from the meadows.

If you love good food, you can cook well. In fact I would go so far as to say you must love food to cook well.

A recipe is rather like a piece of music. Although the notes may be read and reproduced faithfully the result can still be crude, mechanical or just uninteresting. Cooking is primarily a matter of taste, flair and sensibility. One never makes a recipe in precisely the same way for two days running. Sometimes I find myself, heaven knows why, adding a pinch of sugar to a sauce which I have made hundreds of times without sugar, because it suddenly seems absolutely necessary.

If a recipe is a musical composition, it is you who must give it voice. A cook is creative, marrying ingredients in the way a poet marries words, combining flavours, and inventing new and subtle harmonies.

A recipe is not meant to be followed exactly – it is a canvas on which you can embroider. Improvise and invent. Add the zest of this, a drop or two of that, a tiny pinch of the other. Let yourself be led by your palate and your tongue, your eyes and your heart. In other words, be guided by your love of food, and then you will be able to cook.

ROGER VERGÉ

Note to the reader

I have not written this book for professional cooks. Nor have I written it for those in search of new sensations. My recipes have nothing revolutionary about them, and I have not invented anything completely new. Cooking is a matter of interpretation, adaptation, of using what is available, and not of complete innovation. I have collected good traditional recipes from France and elsewhere and have tried to give them my own personal touch, my love of the sun, of happiness and of nature. Above all, I have done my best to make them accessible to all cooks who love good cooking, even if they don't always know all the rules. One thing that is particularly irritating for the non-professional is to have to stop short in the middle of a recipe and search through the book with floury or greasy fingers to 'see page so-and-so' in order to find a particular technique or piece of equipment.

I have therefore tried to make my recipes as complete and detailed as possible, even at the cost of repeating myself. This may make the method section of the recipes rather long, but it also makes them easier to follow. I advise you to read through the entire recipe before starting work.

Take courage, fellow cooks! To your stoves!

For my Tante Célestine
who inspired me with
my love of food

Recipes

Soups

Chilled Artichoke Soup
Crème froide de coeurs d'artichauts

For four people	Comparatively simple Inexpensive *Preparation and cooking time:* 1¼ hours (make in the morning ready to serve in the evening)
Ingredients	5 small purple artichokes **or** 4 large Breton ones 1 chicken stock cube 200 ml (⅓ pint) whipping cream, chilled A small bunch of very fresh parsley, preferably the flat variety which has a better flavour salt
Equipment	1 large saucepan or stewpot holding 7–8 litres (12½–14 pints) food processor, liquidiser or mouli-légumes

At least 6 hours in advance
1 Wash and trim the artichokes. Bring 5 litres (9 pints) of salted water to the boil in the large saucepan. Throw in artichokes and boil rapidly for about 40 minutes, or until you can easily remove one of the outer leaves. Remove them and put to drain heads downwards.

2 Remove the leaves and scrape away the choke at the centre. Only the hearts will be left. They should be quartered and put on one side.

3 Bring $\frac{3}{4}$ litre ($1\frac{1}{2}$ pints) water to the boil in a smaller saucepan. Add the stock cube, allow to boil for 5 minutes, and add the quartered artichoke hearts.

4 Pour the contents of the saucepan into the liquidiser or food processor and blend until you have obtained a perfectly smooth cream. If you use a mouli-légumes strain the resulting cream through a fine wire sieve, pressing down with the back of a ladle. Put the mixture in the refrigerator to chill.

5 Wash the parsley, remove the stalks and chop the leaves finely. Lightly salt the cream and whisk in a chilled bowl until you have a light froth (but not too vigorously, or it will turn into butter).

You will now have prepared
  – the cream of artichokes and stock
  – the salted whipped cream
  – the chopped parsley

6 Stir the artichoke purée and the chopped parsley into the whipped cream. Taste and perfect the flavour with salt and freshly-ground pepper. Pour the soup into the tureen and place in the refrigerator to chill until $\frac{1}{2}$ hour before it is to be eaten.

✳ This is an easy first course, which leaves the cook free for other tasks. It can be served in individual soup bowls.

Little Pots of Chervil Cream
Petite gelée de cerfeuil

For four people   Reasonably simple
Inexpensive
Preparation time: 20 minutes
Infusion and chilling: about 20 hours – it
should therefore be made the day before

Ingredients   5 bunches of freshly-gathered chervil – about
100 g (3½ oz) in all
3 egg yolks
4 tablespoons double cream
salt, pepper

Equipment   1 2-litre (3½-pint) preserving jar with an airtight
lid

Preparing the infusion: one day in advance
1 Separate the sprigs of leaves from the stalks of four of the five bunches of chervil. Put the leaves into the preserving jar. Bring $\frac{3}{4}$ litre ($1\frac{1}{2}$ pints) of very lightly salted water to the boil, plunge in the chervil stalks and allow to simmer gently, uncovered, for 10 minutes. Strain the liquid into the preserving jar and cover immediately with an airtight lid. Leave to infuse for at least 10 hours.

Preparing the cream
2 The next day open the preserving jar and strain the infusion into the saucepan, pressing the leaves with a spoon to extract all their juices. Meanwhile mix together the egg yolks and double cream in a large bowl. Bring the chervil-flavoured liquid to the boil and pour immediately over the egg–cream mixture, whisking all the time. Return the mixture to the saucepan and place over a low heat, stirring all the time. Just before it starts to boil, return the mixture to the bowl and whisk again. Season lightly with salt and pepper and pour into four soup bowls. Chill in the refrigerator for about 4 hours.

Serving the Chervil Cream
3 Just before serving make four little bouquets out of the remaining bunch of chervil, and put one in the centre of each bowl of chervil cream.

✳ This Chervil Cream has all the delicacy and fresh aroma of a beautiful Provençal morning.

Curried Fresh Pea Soup
Soupe de pois frais au curry

For four people	Simple Very inexpensive *Preparation and cooking time:* 45 minutes

Ingredients	1 medium onion – preferably fresh 1 bouquet of flat parsley (which has the best flavour) 1 small lettuce 300 g (10½ oz) shelled fresh peas **or** frozen peas 40 g (1½ oz) butter 5 tablespoons double cream 1 level tablespoon curry powder 1 chicken stock cube 4 slices soft fresh white bread salt

Equipment	1 saucepan holding 3–4 litres (5¼–7 pints) 1 liquidiser or mouli-légumes with a fine blade

1 Slice the onion into fine rounds and cook in half the butter in the saucepan until pale golden – no more. This will take 7–8 minutes. Meanwhile wash the lettuce carefully and chop it coarsely. Add it to the onion in the pan, allow to soften for 2–3 minutes, add the curry powder and stir well.

2 Pour in 1½ litres (2½ pints) hot water, add the stock cube and salt lightly (remembering that the stock cube is already salty). Bring to the boil and cook briskly for 5 minutes. Add the parsley and the peas. Don't cover the pan, whatever you do, because the vegetables must remain very green.

3 While the vegetables are cooking, remove the crusts from the bread and cut each slice into small dice. Fry them with the remaining butter in a frying-pan, stirring well, until they are golden. Drain in a medium sieve and keep hot in a small heated bowl.

4 When the peas are cooked, pour the contents of the saucepan into the liquidiser and blend to a fine cream. If using a mouli-légumes, use the fine blade, and strain the puréed soup through a fine sieve, using a small ladle to push the liquid through.

5 Pour the soup back into the saucepan and reheat. Add 5 tablespoons of cream as it comes to the boil and remove from the heat as soon as it comes back to the boil. Add a pinch of salt if necessary and serve in a tureen with the croûtons in a separate bowl.

Provençal Soup with Pistou
Soupe au pistou

For six people
Simple
Very inexpensive
Preparation time: 12 hours to soak the beans,
  if dried; 40 minutes preparation
Cooking and serving: 45 minutes

Ingredients
300 g (10½ oz) fresh white coco beans or 200 g
  (7 oz) dried white coco beans (these are
  rounder than haricot beans. They can be
  obtained from Italian grocers. If you cannot
  find them use haricot beans)
1 handsome potato weighing 100 g (3½ oz)
2 carrots
2 turnips
2 slender courgettes
2 inner stalks of celery
1 good handful of French beans
The white part of a leek
1 onion preferably fresh
4 large ripe tomatoes weighing 80 g (3 oz) each
30 fresh basil leaves
6 cloves of garlic
8 generous tablespoons olive oil
2 beef or chicken stock cubes
1 bouquet garni containing a sprig of thyme,
  a bayleaf and four sprigs of parsley, tied with
  a thread
salt and pepper

Equipment
1 stewpot or marmite holding 6–7 litres (10½–
  12½ pints)
1 pestle and mortar **or** a liquidiser

Recommended wines
Tavel rosé or any young Provençal rosé, cool
but not iced

Soaking the beans: a day in advance
1 If you are using dried beans put them to soak in cold water for
12 hours.

Preparing the soup base

2 Wash and peel the various vegetables in cold water, without leaving them to soak for too long.

3 Put the soaked haricots on to boil, in 2 litres (3½ pints) cold water, together with the bouquet garni. Add salt after the water has boiled for 5 minutes. They will take about 1 hour to cook, but test them from time to time. If you are using fresh haricots they will only take 30 minutes; test them occasionally in the same way. When the beans are cooked, set them aside in their cooking water to keep hot.

4 Cut the carrots, turnips, courgettes and onion into 1 cm (½ inch) dice and cut the French beans into 1 cm (½ inch) lengths (don't try to dice these!) Slice the leek and celery finely. Put all the vegetables (except the haricots) into the stewpot with 4 tablespoons olive oil and the same quantity of cold water. Soften over a medium heat for 10 minutes, stirring constantly. During this time the vegetables will first release and then re-absorb their juices giving the soup a good flavour without losing their own. After 10 minutes there should be no water left, but the vegetables should not have started to brown.

5 Pour 4 litres (7 pints) of cold water over the vegetables and add 2 stock cubes. Bring to the boil over a brisk heat and add salt after boiling for 5 minutes. Meanwhile cut the peeled potato into 1 cm (½ inch) dice and throw them into the soup after it has been boiling for 20 minutes. Make sure that the liquid does not reduce too much: if it does, add a little of the cooking water from the haricot beans. Allow to boil away while you prepare the pistou.

Preparing the tomatoes and basil

6 While the soup is cooking, peel and halve the tomatoes. Press each half in the palm of your hand to squeeze out the pips and excess juice. Cut them into 1 cm (½ inch) dice. Peel the cloves of garlic and remove the stalks from the basil.

7 *If you are using a mortar*, crush the cloves of garlic and the basil thoroughly with the pestle. Add the diced tomatoes (6) and pound

the whole mixture together until it is a fine paste without any lumps. Add the remaining 4 tablespoons of olive oil and stir it in carefully with the pestle. Season with a few turns of the pepper-mill.

If you are using a liquidiser, or food-processor, first purée the garlic and basil with 2 tablespoons of olive oil. Then, add the tomato dice (6) and blend, pouring the rest of the olive oil. Season with a few turns of the pepper-mill.

Finishing and serving the soup

8 You now have three elements: the cooked haricot beans (3), the soup with its vegetables (4) and the 'ointment' of garlic, basil, tomato and oil (6). Remove the bouquet garni from the haricots. Add them with their cooking liquid to the stewpot containing the vegetable soup. Bring to the boil briefly and add salt if necessary. Away from direct heat, stir in the 'pistou' with a wooden spoon, without letting the soup re-boil. Carry it straight to the table, where the marvellous aroma will have preceded you.

✳ This soup can be cooked in advance, provided you leave the addition of the 'pistou' till the very last moment. It can be served hot, warm or cold, but never chilled.

✳ None of the vegetables I have suggested are indispensable and they can be replaced by others. For example, petits pois can be substituted for French beans, marrow for courgettes; the haricot beans and potato can be omitted in favour of small pasta shells. I have even enjoyed a soupe au pistou without vegetables of any kind, made by my friend Toinette in her small village in the Var. Needing to prepare a meal at very short notice, she simply softened a chopped onion in olive oil, added 2 litres (3½ pints) of water and brought it to the boil before adding 200 g (7 oz) of pasta shells. To finish the soup, she added a superb pistou made of 4 large tomatoes, a bunch of basil, 2 cloves of garlic, 5 tablespoons of olive oil and a twist of the pepper-mill. What could be simpler. This kind of simplicity is always best when you are entertaining your real friends, the ones you love and who love you too. The people of Provence make the best friends in the world, (and they know how to make friends with other people from less fortunate places).

Almond Cream Soup
Crème au lait d'amandes

For four people	Absolutely simple
	Inexpensive
	Preparation time: 1 hour

Ingredients 20 g ($\frac{3}{4}$ oz) butter
the white part of 1 leek
2 chicken stock cubes
100 g ($3\frac{1}{2}$ oz) ground almonds such as you can
  buy for pâtisserie
10 g ($\frac{1}{3}$ oz) round-grain Carolina rice
300 ml ($\frac{1}{2}$ pint) whipping cream
2 egg yolks
salt

Equipment 1 liquidiser or mouli-légumes with a fine blade
1 fine sieve

1 Wash and drain the rice. Peel and wash the white part of the leek and cut it into fine rounds. Put the sliced leek into the saucepan with the butter and 1 tablespoon water, and soften for 5 minutes over a gentle heat. Then add 1 litre ($1\frac{3}{4}$ pints) water, bring to the boil and add the stock cubes, the rice and the ground almonds. Cover and cook over a very low heat for 25 minutes.

2 Meanwhile, whisk the cream and the egg yolks together in the large bowl. Liquidise the soup (1) or sieve through the fine blade of the mouli-légumes, and add to the cream, whisking all the time. Return everything to the saucepan and re-heat over a gentle heat, removing the pan immediately at the first signs of boiling. Season with salt and strain through a fine wire sieve. Serve in hot soup cups or bowls.

Fresh Tomato Soup
Crème de tomates fraîches

For two people Simple
Inexpensive
Preparation time: 45 minutes

Ingredients 400 g (14½ oz) very ripe tomatoes
1 onion weighing 120 g (4¼ oz), preferably fresh
1 small sprig of thyme
½ clove of garlic
1 chicken stock cube
15 g (½ oz) butter
5 tablespoons whipping cream
1 egg yolk
1 pinch caster sugar
salt, pepper

Equipment 1 liquidiser or mouli-légumes

1 Peel the onion and slice finely. Put it in a large saucepan with the butter and 2 tablespoons of water. Cook and soften over a low heat for 10–15 minutes, without browning the onion.

2 Wash the tomatoes and remove their stalks. Cut each one into four or six pieces and add to the softened onion (1) together with the chopped clove of garlic, thyme and sugar. Increase the heat and let the tomatoes melt and soften for about 10 minutes (stirring with a wooden spoon). While the tomatoes are cooking, bring ¼ litre (scant half-pint) of water to the boil and dissolve the bouillon cube in it. Add this liquid to the tomatoes and boil for 2–3 minutes.

3 Remove the sprig of thyme and pour the contents of the saucepan (2) into the liquidiser jar or through a mouli-légumes placed over a saucepan. Purée or sieve thoroughly. Strain through the wire sieve, return to the saucepan and bring to the boil.

4 Meanwhile, whisk the 5 tablespoons of cream and the egg yolk together in a large bowl. When the tomato mixture has reached the boil, pour it into the bowl and whisk thoroughly.

5 Return the contents of the bowl to the saucepan and place over a gentle heat, whisking all the time. Remove the pan just before the soup comes to the boil. Whisk for a further 2 minutes away from the heat. Taste, and add the necessary salt and pepper. Strain the soup through a fine sieve into a tureen and serve immediately.

✳ You can add something to this soup by serving it in large soup plates or bowls, and at the last moment floating a spoonful of lightly-whipped salted cream in the middle of each. Finish with a sprinkling of chopped chervil.

Caribbean Soup
Crème Antillaise

For four people Very simple
Inexpensive
Preparation time: 50 minutes

Ingredients 2 medium-size fresh onions
400 g (14½ oz) leaf spinach (New Zealand spinach can be used instead)
30 g (1 oz) butter
70 g (2½ oz) round-grain Carolina rice
6 tablespoons double cream
3 tablespoons dried and grated coconut
1 beef stock cube
salt, pepper, nutmeg

Equipment 1 liquidiser or mouli-légumes
1 nutmeg grater
1 fine strainer

1 Peel the onions and slice finely. Remove the central stalks from the spinach leaves and wash in several waters. Drain in the colander.

2 Put the sliced onion into the saucepan with the butter, and soften for about 10 minutes, stirring with a wooden spoon. The onions should be barely golden: on no account let them brown. Add 1½ litres (2½ pints) hot water and bring to the boil. Sprinkle in the rice in a fine shower, then add the grated coconut. Allow to cook over a moderate heat for 20 minutes, then add the well-drained spinach and the stock cube. Bring to the boil again and cook for a further 5 minutes. Add salt, and a generous grating of nutmeg.

3 Purée the soup in the liquidiser or sieve through the fine blade of the mouli-légumes. Then, strain back into the pan through a wire sieve, pressing the liquid through with the back of a small ladle.

4 Add the cream, and bring back to the boil. Season with five or six turns of the pepper-mill and add salt if necessary. Serve in a tureen. The soup should be a beautiful pale green colour.

✱ In the French West Indies they serve a peasant soup called Calalou or Kalalou, which also happens to be the name of a plant resembling New Zealand spinach. It is made with a beef bouillon thickened with rice in which the Calalou leaves are cooked. It is finished with fresh coconut juice, pressed from freshly-grated coconut. The same soup, generously seasoned with ground pepper, is called 'pepper-pot' in Jamaica. This Caribbean Soup is adapted from these recipes, but calls for ingredients that are less difficult to find.

Fish Soup from the Moulin de Mougins
Soupe de poissons du Moulin

For eight people	Relatively simple Expensive *Preparation time:* 15 minutes *Cooking time:* 1 hour

Ingredients 2 kg (4½ lb) rock fish, freshly caught. If you live on the Mediterranean coast, where this recipe can really be made properly, the fishermen can provide the ingredients for this soup. Generally, these will include small rascasse, rouquiers and girelles (members of the wrasse family), galinettes, small shore crabs of the kind called favouilles, and small crustaceans. A few slices of moray eel (murène) are also not to be despised, and will add to the richness of the soup.
The most important thing is that the fishes should not be gutted, scaled or beheaded. Don't wash them, either.
300 g (10½ oz) onions
1 small whole head of garlic
5 large ripe tomatoes
4 dried fennel branches
2 sprigs of thyme
1 bayleaf
150 ml (¼ pint) olive oil
¼ teaspoon whole saffron stamens
salt, pepper

Equipment 1 mouli-légumes
1 fine wire sieve

Recommended wines all Provençal white wines

1 Peel the onions and slice finely. Cut the tomatoes into eight pieces each. Cut the whole head of garlic in two, horizontally.

2 Soften the onions in the olive oil in the large saucepan, and let them turn golden over a brisk heat, stirring with a wooden spoon. Keeping it over a fierce heat, put the fish in the pan and then add garlic, tomatoes and herbs and mix all together well. Let all the ingredients sweat for about 10 minutes.

3 Pour 5 litres (8¾ pints) water into the saucepan and bring to the boil. Without reducing the heat, cook at a galloping boil for 15–25 minutes. Then, and only then, add the salt, pepper and saffron.

4 Pass the contents of the saucepan through the coarse blade of the mouli-légumes placed over the other saucepan, having first fished out the herbs. It will be hard going, but keep working away, and eventually everything will go through.

5 Bring to the boil again, and, just before serving, strain through a conical wire strainer, held in your left hand over the hot soup tureen (unless you are left-handed, in which case it will be the other way round). With your right hand, pump up and down with a small ladle to extract as much as possible of this marvellous soup. Forget Rouille or grated cheese: this dish is eaten simply with thin slices of French bread rubbed with garlic.

✳ If you don't want to serve the soup immediately it has been strained for the last time (5), keep it in a cold place in an airtight container. When you are ready to eat, just heat it through and all its flavour and fragrance will be restored.

✳ It won't matter if the sun doesn't come out when you serve this soup, because it's hotter than the sunshine of the Midi.
Even so, I will give another fish soup, for Parisians this time – which means to a Provençal anyone who lives north of Aix-en-Provence . . . they aren't really that bad, just different, so let them have their own soup too.
Sure enough, you will find some of the flavours of Provence in it, but it isn't quite the same thing . . . anyway it is still extremely good, this Parisian fish soup.

Parisian Fish Soup
Soupe de poissons Parisienne

For eight people	Fairly simple Moderately expensive *Preparation time:* 30 minutes *Cooking time:* 1 hour

---

Ingredients 2½ kg (5½ lb) fresh fish, which *must* include whiting and can include red mullet, slices of conger eel, small monkfish, small crabs, and gurhards
300 g (10½ oz) onions, finely chopped
1 small whole head of garlic
5 large ripe tomatoes
5 dried fennel twigs (yes, that's one more than usual)
2 sprigs of thyme
1 bayleaf
150 ml (¼ pint) olive oil
¼ teaspoon whole saffron stamens
salt, pepper

Equipment 1 saucepan holding 8–10 litres (14–18 pints), as shallow as possible in order to present the maximum area to the fire
1 mouli-légumes
1 fine conical sieve

Recommended wines any white wine from Provence or from the Côtes du Rhône

---

Preparation

1 Scale, gut, wash and drain the various fish.

2 Peel the onions and slice them finely into rounds.

3 Cut the tomatoes into eight pieces each. Cut the head of garlic into two, horizontally.

Cooking the soup

4 Soften the onions in the olive oil in the large saucepan and let them turn golden over a brisk heat, stirring constantly with a wooden spoon. Then, still over a fierce heat, pile the fish into the pan. Add the garlic, tomatoes and herbs and mix everything together well. Allow the fish and vegetables to sweat for 10 minutes, releasing their juices, then add 5 litres ($8\frac{1}{4}$ pints) cold water.

5 Still over a fierce heat, bring the soup back to the boil and cook uncovered at a galloping boil for 15–20 minutes. Only then add the salt, pepper and saffron, and sieve through the mouli-légumes. Keep working away and everything except the herbs will go through – fish, tomatoes, garlic. Return to the saucepan and re-boil. Just before serving strain the soup through a fine conical sieve, pressing it through firmly with the back of a small ladle, which you pump rapidly up and down.

6 If you do not want to serve the soup immediately, set it aside in a cool place. When you are ready to eat it re-heating will bring out its marvellous and mouth-watering fragrance.

✱ Your success will depend on the choice and freshness of your fish, which should be small specimens with rosy gills, clear eyes, shining scales and firm flesh.

✱ With this Parisian soup you will naturally be expected to serve a Rouille, and even more certainly croûtons rubbed with garlic. A recipe for Rouille follows.

Rouille

For eight people Simple
Very cheap
Preparation time: 10 minutes

Ingredients 5 cm (2 inches) of a French baguette loaf
1 egg yolk
6 tablespoons olive oil
4 cloves of garlic
1 pinch whole saffron stamens
6 tablespoons hot fish soup (see preceding recipe)
salt, pepper

Equipment a pestle and mortar **or** a liquidiser **or** food-processor

1 Cut the bread into cubes and soak in the fish soup. Put them in a bowl and work to a paste.

2 Crush the garlic to a fine purée in the mortar, and add the saffron, the egg yolk and the bread mixture (1). Work the mixture well. Then, using a circular movement of the pestle, incorporate the oil, salt and pepper as if making a mayonnaise. If the mixture turns oily or curdles, add two large tablespoons of hot fish soup and continue to stir.

3 If you are using a liquidiser or food-processor, follow the same method at the lowest possible speed. Serve in a sauceboat or bowl, and spread on rounds of French bread, which are then floated in the bowls of soup.

Light
First
Courses

The Different Varieties of Green Salad
Their seasons and seasonings

Salad is a dish that has its place at every meal and in all climates. No matter what the plants are, and whatever seasonings and dressings are chosen, a salad always adds a note of gaiety, a feeling of freshness and being close to nature.

In *The Physiology of Taste* Brillat-Savarin tells us that 'a salad rejoices the heart'. He might well have added 'and the palate, the eyes ... and the stomach'.

Cultivated Dandelion (*Barbe de capucin*), November–April. A type of chicory with denticulated leaves, forced in sand, in dark cellars or under straw. Seasoning: walnut oil.

Batavian endive (*Batavia*), May–November. Very tender when young, Batavia becomes crisp and delicately crimped, with a colour ranging from pale gold to dark green, edged with red-brown. Seasoning: olive oil.

Curly endive (*Chicorée frisée*), March–May. A very crisp variety, green, with a white heart.

Curly endive (*Chicorée frisée*), September–December. A white variety, only slightly curly. Seasoning: walnut oil.

Cornette, December–March. A variety similar to curly endive in its faintly bitter taste. The leaves are crisp and very dark green, turning reddish with the first frost. Seasoning: walnut oil.

Watercress (*Cresson*), March–December. Unmistakable for its peppery flavour. This plant is only happy with its feet in the water and with abundant shade to protect it from the heat of summer. Seasoning: olive oil.

Chicory (*Endive*), October–April. A shade-loving plant which is grown in the dark, either buried in sand or more commonly in cellars. Most chicory comes from Belgium, and is known there as 'witloof'. Seasoning: olive oil.

Lettuce (*Laitue*), March–December. The most common of all salad plants, and one that comes in many different varieties. I think that the delicately flavoured beautiful green lettuces without a pronounced heart are preferable to the pale varieties with firm hearts, which to me lack flavour. Seasoning: olive oil, or just cream and lemon juice.

Lamb's Lettuce, Corn Salad (*Mâche*), end November–April. In the Midi this is also called doucette or boursette. It is cultivated commercially but also grows wild. It becomes darker green after the first frosts, and its slightly pungent taste becomes subdued and more delicate. Seasoning: olive oil.

Mesclun, all the year round. Mesclun is not an individual salad plant but an amazing mixture of several different kinds. Originally it was made up of wild herbs: rocket (*riquette*), dandelions (*pissenlit*), lamb's lettuce (*mâche*), purslane (*pourpier*), wild chicory, etc. I have even found chickweed (*senneson*), that small yellow-flowered weed that is generally kept for canaries. Today mesclun is usually made up of a number of small cultivated salad plants, varying according to the time of year. Commonly used are: curly endive, Batavia, cornette, lamb's lettuce, dandelions, escarole, red endive (*radicchio trevisano*), chervil, parsley and even fennel. This salad is mostly eaten between Cannes and Menton and each village has its own variation. Seasoning: olive oil, of course.

Dandelion (*Pissenlit*), end November–March. This is a salad that you must know how to find. The easiest way of tracking it down is to look for the bright yellow flowers that push their way up through the grass of the meadows. That's what I used to do when my mother sent me out to find the salad for the evening meal. My basket was filled quick as a wink, and I was free to go off and play with my friends. When I got home the dressing-down was not for the salad but for me, and the supper had gone to the rabbits. This was because dandelions should not be eaten when in flower. They should be picked after a frost and chosen as small as possible. You can also pick leaves from those tight rosettes showing only the promise of a flower which reminds me of the winder of an old man's pocket watch. To close the discussion of dandelions I must tell you the disgusting fact that the best and tenderest are found under dried cowpats or beneath mole-hills. Seasoning: walnut oil.

Escarole, Batavian endive (*scarole*), September–February. This is a robust, somewhat leathery salad with a touch of bitterness. It stands up well to frost, becoming slightly russet-coloured round the edges of the leaves. Seasoning: olive oil.

Cos lettuce (*Romaine*), June–September. This beautiful salad stands tall and straight. Its shiny crisp leaves are so brittle that my Aunt Célestine refused to submit them to the ordeal of washing and the salad basket. She took off the leaves one by one, and wiped them delicately with a cloth – a real act of love. Seasoning: olive oil.

Red chicory (*Radicchio Trevisano, Trevise*), October–April. This superb salad is usually eaten only with other salads such as lamb's lettuce and curly endive. It is deep orchid purple, crisp and very bitter. Frost is good for it and turns it a still darker hue. Seasoning: olive oil.

(A note on salad dressings appears on pages 90–91)

Cucumber Salad with Chervil

Salade de concombres à la crème de cerfeuil

For two people   Simple
Inexpensive
Preparation time: salting the cucumbers, 3
  hours; finishing the salad, 15 minutes

Ingredients   2 cucumbers
3 tablespoons coarse salt
2 tablespoons well chilled double cream
½ teaspoon Dijon mustard
juice of one lemon
3 tablespoons roughly-chopped chervil
salt, pepper

1 Peel the cucumbers thinly with a potato-peeler. Cut them in half lengthways, and hollow out the seeds with a teaspoon. Then, slice the cucumber halves as finely as possible. Put the slices in a bowl and cover them with 3 tablespoons of coarse salt (fine salt would do instead). Mix in well and leave for at least 2½ hours. The quantity of salt may seem enormous to you but it will remove all the surplus water from the cucumbers and will be strained off with the water when they are drained.

2 Meanwhile, prepare the cream sauce. Put the chilled cream, mustard and lemon juice in a bowl and whip till thick and foamy. Add the chervil and 3 or 4 turns of the pepper-mill. When you are whipping the cream, do not overdo it or you will end up with butter. When the cream clings to the wires of the whisk or to the beater, it is time to stop.

3 Put the cucumbers to drain in a colander, pressing them down to get rid of all the liquid. Mix them into the whipped cream, taste for seasoning and serve very cold.

Saddle of Rabbit Salad with Mesclun

Salade de râble de lapereau aux feuilles de mesclun

For two people	Fairly simple Moderately expensive *Preparation time:* 60 minutes

Ingredients	The saddle of a young rabbit weighing about 2 kg (4½ lb) with its liver (use the rest of the rabbit for Rabbit in Jelly, page 67) 100 g (3½ oz) lard, **or**, better still, goose fat or duck fat 70 g (2½ oz) butter 2 handfuls of mixed salads (radicchio trevisano, lamb's lettuce, curly endive, cos lettuce, escarole and, if you are in Provence, a mixture of wild herbs) (see page 46) 200 g (7 oz) white button mushrooms 1 very ripe tomato weighing 150 g (5½ oz) salt, pepper 1 tablespoon chopped chervil

Optional
8 asparagus spears
60 g (2 oz) duck foie gras
2 slices of black truffle

Equipment	1 small enamelled cast-iron cocotte large enough to hold the saddle a very thin, very sharp, knife 1 skewer

Recommended wines	dry white wines, for instance dry Graves, Côtes du Rhône, Côtes de Provence

✳ I sometimes replace the chervil in the butter dressing with a tablespoon of fresh chopped truffle. It obviously couldn't be other than delicious, but it certainly isn't obligatory.

1 Remove the gall from the centre of the rabbit's liver. Season the liver with salt and pepper and put it in a small saucepan with the lard over a very slow heat for 15–20 minutes. Keep on one side on a plate.

2 Separate the saddle, which is the part between the last rib and the tops of the hind legs. Remove the skin flaps from the sides and, using a very sharp knife, cut away the fine transparent membrane that covers the pale flesh of the saddle. Season with salt and pepper and lay the saddle in the cocotte with 20 g ($\frac{3}{4}$ oz) butter. Cover and cook for 20 minutes on a very slow heat, making certain that the meat remains pale and that the butter stays creamy-white. The rabbit is perfectly cooked when a trussing needle or skewer pushed into the flesh produces a bead of transparent colourless liquid.

3 While the rabbit cooks, you will have time to wash and dry the salads. Next plunge the tomato in boiling water for 2 minutes and then put it immediately under the cold tap so that it will be easy to peel. Cut it in half and press each half in the palm of your hand to squeeze out excess moisture and seeds. Chop coarsely. If you are using fresh asparagus cook it for 15 minutes. Wash the mushrooms and slice them finely.

4 Slice the rabbit liver very finely into long slices and keep hot. Slice the saddle (parallel with the backbone) in long, thin pieces, and keep hot. Take two warm soup plates and put a layer of well-dried salad in each, followed by a layer of fine mushroom slices. Arrange slices of the rabbit liver over one side of each salad and slices of saddle on the other. Place a little posy of chopped tomato in the centre of each. If you are using asparagus, foie gras or truffles arrange them in the middle in the same way. Keep the salads warm while you prepare the dressing.

5 Put the cocotte with its cooking juices back on the heat. Add 3 tablespoons of water and a pinch of salt. Bring to the boil and add 50 g ($1\frac{3}{4}$ oz) unsalted butter whisking vigorously to make an emulsion of water and butter. Remove the cocotte from the heat and stir in a tablespoon of chopped chervil. Sprinkle the salads lightly with salt and pepper, then divide the hot butter evenly between them. Serve immediately.

Salad of French Beans with Hazelnuts

Salade de haricots verts à la crème et aux noisettes

For two people	Simple
	Inexpensive
	Preparation time: 10 minutes
	Cooking time: 7–8 minutes

Ingredients
400 g (14¼ oz) French beans
20 g (¾ oz) shelled hazelnuts
2 tablespoons chopped chervil (optional)
1 teaspoon strong Dijon mustard
juice of ½ lemon
4 tablespoons chilled double cream
4 pale lettuce leaves
salt, pepper

Equipment
1 saucepan holding 5–6 litres (8¾–10½ pints)
1 large bowl, chilled in the refrigerator

✳ It is vital to choose exceptionally fresh French beans. To test for freshness you need only break one in half. If it snaps cleanly and crisply it is fresh; if it bends, and seems to stretch, it is not. Ideally, you should look for the smallest beans, about the size of the prong of a large fork, with some of their white flowers still attached. Watch them carefully while they cook as they will only need about 4–5 minutes boiling. If you can't get the finest, you should still choose beans that are fresh enough to snap in half.

✳ French beans should not be cooked more than 2 hours before they are to be eaten, or they will wilt.

1 Top and tail the beans in the usual way. Wash them and drain in a colander. Bring 3 litres (5¼ pints) of water with 2 tablespoons of coarse salt to the boil and throw in the beans. Do not cover. When they have cooked for 4–5 minutes take one out from time to time and test it between your teeth to see if it is done. (It is impossible to give an exact cooking time because so much depends on the calcium content of the water and above all on the quality of the beans.) Meanwhile, get ready a bowl of cold water and ice cubes. When the beans are still just slightly crisp, drain them quickly and plunge into the cold water. This operation stops the cooking and keeps them beautifully green. Drain carefully, if necessary drying them on a cloth, and keep in a cool place.

2 Cut the hazelnuts into thin slices with a small sharp knife and toast lightly in a small cast-iron frying pan over a brisk heat, stirring all the time. They should not brown, but remain pale. This operation can also be done in the oven (or under an ordinary grill). Put the nuts on a plate to cool.

3 Take the chilled bowl out of the refrigerator, and put the chilled cream, mustard, lemon juice, salt and pepper into it. Whisk lightly to mix the ingredients thoroughly, then add the chopped chervil (if used) and the beans. Turn the beans over in the cream with a spoon. Taste the dressing and add salt if necessary. This operation should not be carried out more than half an hour before the meal.

4 In each of two deep plates put two lettuce leaves like open hands. Pile the beans, in their dressing, on the lettuce in two mounds, and finish with a sprinkling of grilled hazelnuts (2). Serve.

Crab Salad with Grapefruit
Salade de pamplemousse au crabe

For two people   Fairly simple
Moderately expensive
Preparation time: using fresh crab, 45 minutes;
   with tinned crab, 25 minutes

Ingredients   2 grapefruits, pink for preference as they are
   usually sweeter
1 lettuce heart
1 live or freshly-cooked crab weighing 800 g
   (1¾ lb) **or** a 100 g (3½ oz) tin of Russian or
   Alaskan crabmeat
5 tablespoons double cream
2 teaspoons tomato ketchup
1 tablespoon cognac
a pinch of cayenne pepper **or** three drops Tabasco
salt
bayleaves for decoration

Recommended   dry white – Côtes de Provence or Cassis
wines

1 *With a live crab:* Cook for 25 minutes in salted boiling water, then allow to cool. Remove the claws and crack them carefully, without crushing them, with the back of a heavy knife. Extract the flesh. Open the body and discard the inedible parts. Pick out all the meat, and remove any little membranes or pieces of shell. Set aside on a plate.
With tinned crab: Pick over the crabmeat and discard any membranes or pieces of shell and set aside on a plate.

2 Peel the grapefruit with a sharp knife, taking care to cut away all the white pith. Hold the peeled fruit over a plate and insert a thin sharp knife between both sides of the membrane and the flesh of each segment or 'pig', in such a way that the flesh drops out and the inner membranes remain attached to the central core of the fruit. Remove the pips, and keep the skinned segments and juice on one side in the plate.
Wash the lettuce heart, detaching one leaf at a time, and dry carefully in a cloth.

3 In a bowl mix the cream, the tomato ketchup, the cognac and 4 tablespoons of the grapefruit juice which has collected in the plate (2). Add a pinch of salt and cayenne pepper, or salt and 3 drops of Tabasco. Whisk until the mixture becomes thick and foamy, but take care not to beat for too long or the sauce will turn granular.

4 Line the edges of two plates with bayleaves (*not to be eaten*) and arrange the well-drained grapefruit segments (2) over them. Place the lettuce leaves in the centre of the plates and scatter the crabmeat (1) on top, coat with the sauce (3) and serve very cold.

Mikado Salad

Salade Mikado

For two people	Simple
	Moderately expensive
	Preparation time: 25 minutes

Ingredients
1 avocado pear weighing about 180 g (6½ oz)
1 heart of a frizzy or curly endive
350 g (12½ oz) firm red tomatoes
2 large white mushrooms (about 80 g (3 oz) each)
1 tablespoon red wine vinegar
½ teaspoon Dijon mustard
3 tablespoons olive oil
20 g (¾ oz) truffles cut in tiny julienne strips (optional)
salt, pepper

✽ This salad doesn't set out to be grand but it brings together ingredients of similarly delicate taste and texture. This is all that is needed to achieve a great dish. And what is Japanese about this Mikado Salad? Not much, in fact, but at the time I thought of it I left the making of it to one of my chefs, who happened to be Japanese. As his name was unpronounceable I always called him 'Mikado'. That's all there is to it.

1 Bring 1 litre (1¾ pints) of water to the boil in a saucepan. Remove the stalks and plunge the tomatoes into the boiling water for 2 minutes. Then run them under the cold tap. They will now be very easy to peel. Cut each in two and press the halves in the palm of your hand to squeeze out the pips and excess juice. Cut the tomatoes into small dice and set aside in a colander. Wash and dry the endive carefully.

2 Cut the avocado in two lengthwise and remove the skin – it should come away easily if the avocado is perfectly ripe. Cut the flesh into thin slices and set aside on a plate. (If you are doing this in advance, keep the stone and put it with the avocado slices on a plate under a covering of plastic wrap. This helps prevent the avocado flesh darkening.) Take the tops of the two mushrooms, keeping the stalks for another use, wash and dry them and slice thinly.

3 To arrange the salad, put a tuft of endive in the middle of each plate. The rest of each plate is divided into three parts – the first being filled with the drained dice of tomato, the second with the slices of mushroom and the third with the slices of avocado. If you are using truffle julienne, sprinkle them over the tufts of endive.

4 Mix the wine vinegar and mustard in a bowl. Season with salt and pepper, add the olive oil and mix thoroughly. Season the salads with salt and pepper and sprinkle the vinaigrette over them with a spoon. Serve chilled.

Salad of Quails with Wild Mushrooms

Salade de cailles aux champignons des bois

For two people	Simple Moderately expensive *Preparation time:* 45 minutes

Ingredients	200 g (7 oz) lamb's lettuce (mâche) **or** Batavian endive 200 g (7 oz) wood mushrooms (chanterelles) 2 plump quails a small bouquet of chives, parsley and chervil, finely chopped 1 teaspoon of strong Dijon mustard 2 tablespoons red wine vinegar 5 tablespoons olive oil 15 g ($\frac{1}{2}$ oz) butter salt, pepper

Recommended wines	red – Côtes du Rhône or Beaujolais

1 Preheat the oven to 250°C/500°F/Mark 10. Wash and drain the salads and the chanterelles. Heat 1 tablespoon of olive oil in a frying-pan over a brisk heat and when the oil is smoking throw in the mushrooms. Sauté them rapidly for 3–4 minutes and drain in a colander.

2 Pluck and gut the quails, if it has not already been done, and season them inside and out with salt and pepper. Place them in a small roasting-tin with 15 g ($\frac{1}{2}$ oz) butter, and roast in the hot oven for 15 minutes. When they are done, bone the quails with a small sharp knife and put the meat on one side to keep warm.

3 Discard the butter in which the quails have cooked and pour 2 tablespoons of wine vinegar into the still-warm roasting-tin. Place over a moderate heat and simmer briefly, scraping up the juices and caramelised deposits. Pour immediately into a bowl and add the mustard, salt and pepper and then the 4 remaining tablespoons of olive oil. Mix thoroughly together with a small whisk. Taste for seasoning and add the finely-chopped herbs.

4 Season the greenery, washed and dried, with a tablespoon of the vinaigrette (3) and arrange round the edges of two warm plates. Pile up the mushrooms, similarly dressed with vinaigrette, in the middle, and top with the quail meat cut into fine slices. Serve the rest of the dressing separately. This rather leisurely process means that the salad is served warm rather than hot.

✳ It can equally well be served cold and be prepared a short time in advance. In any case you must on no account put the quail meat or the chanterelles in the refrigerator, or season the green salad till the last moment.

Anchoïade
L'anchoïade

For fifteen people (Anchoïade keeps well in an airtight jar so you can make enough for several meals)
Simple
Moderately expensive
Preparation time: with a liquidiser, 15 minutes; with a mouli-légumes, 25 minutes

Ingredients 300 g (10½ oz) tinned anchovy fillets in olive oil
1 litre (1¾ pints) finest first-pressing (virgin) olive oil
6 cloves of garlic, chopped
2 teaspoons thyme
3 tablespoons chopped basil
3 tablespoons Dijon mustard
3 tablespoons red wine vinegar
1 teaspoon ground pepper

Recommended wines young and fresh – red, white or rosé from Provence

1 *With a liquidiser or food-processor:* Put all the ingredients listed above into the container and run the machine until you have a smooth purée. (For most domestic liquidisers and mixers these quantities will have to be processed in two batches.)

2 *With a mouli-légumes:* Warm (they should only be warm not hot) the anchovies with 3 tablespoons olive oil in a shallow pan, dissolving the fillets with a wooden spoon. Then place the mouli-légumes over a large bowl and, adding a little olive oil from time to time to ease the process, sieve the anchovies, together with the chopped garlic, chopped basil and thyme, through the fine blade. Scrape off and add to the rest any purée which may be clinging to the blade when you have finished. Add the mustard, vinegar, pepper and the remaining olive oil to the bowl and work well with a whisk to obtain a smooth purée. Serve in the same bowl.

✳ Anchoïade can be served with large hot slices of toasted pain de campagne or other French bread, and with salad, for example mesclun (see page 47), black olives, quartered tomatoes, hard-boiled eggs. Serve in a bowl or terrine large enough for all the guests to dip their vegetables in.
La Grande Anchoïade as I serve it at the Moulin is a meal in itself. Alongside the slices of toasted bread serve a basket of raw vegetables – crudités – of all kinds: tomatoes, mushrooms, celery, radishes, Florence fennel, cucumbers, peppers, lettuce hearts, tiny artichokes, spring onions, fresh broad beans, quarters of lemons, hard-boiled eggs, black olives from Nice, etc. It is particularly important to serve the wine cool and abundantly and to place the table in the shade of a large tree. The dish is already suffused with sunshine and leads to thoughts of a siesta....

✳ If you use only part of the quantity of sauce specified in this recipe, store the rest in a wide-mouthed airtight preserving jar in the refrigerator. Take it out 30 minutes before you want to serve it.

Tapenade

Simple
Inexpensive
Preparation time: 30 minutes
Keeps: 3 months in the refrigerator

Ingredients	500 g (1 lb 2 oz) large black olives 1 clove of garlic 100 g (3½ oz) anchovy fillets preserved in oil 50 g (1¾ oz) capers preserved in vinegar 3 tablespoons olive oil pepper
Special equipment	1 liquidiser or food-processor or (if you are brave) a pestle and mortar several small wide-mouthed preserving jars with a total capacity of 500 g (1 lb 2 oz) 1 olive (or cherry) stoner
Recommended wines	any product of the vine, provided it is cool, young and drinkable

1 Remove the stones from the olives. This is most easily done with an olive stoner but if you don't have one crush the olives, but not the stones, with a heavy knife and remove the stones. Put the stoned olives in the mixer or the mortar and add the anchovy fillets, the clove of garlic, peeled and crushed, and the carefully drained capers. Finally, add the olive oil and several turns of the pepper-mill. With a liquidiser or food processor simply blend the ingredients for 5 minutes. With a mortar it's a very different kettle of fish and you will have to wield the pestle with a terrific energy – but the result will be worth it.

2 To store tapenade, several small jars are better than one large one. Press the mixture well down and cover with a thin layer of olive oil. Put on airtight lids and keep in the refrigerator or a very cool place.

Uses
As an aperitif, spread on slices of toasted French bread, as an hors d'œuvre, served with raw vegetables (crudités) and hard-boiled eggs; with a salad (dressed with olive oil, naturally) served on little slices of toasted bread which may be rubbed with garlic; in a sandwich – a stick of French bread split in half and lightly toasted, then filled with slices of tomato, hard-boiled eggs, spring onions and a few anchovy fillets and spread with tapenade; for pure greed – on slices of toast with goats' cheese preserved in oil (see recipe, page 242).

✳ Tapenade is one of those delicacies that give one pleasure whenever one opens the refrigerator door, either to allay a momentary pang of hunger or to satisfy a sudden surge of greed.

Tante Célestine's Beef Nougat
Nougat de boeuf de ma tante Célestine

For six to eight people

Can be difficult
Moderately expensive
Preparation time: 1 hour
Marination time: 4 hours
Cooking time: 5 hours
Chilling and finishing time: 8 hours
N.B. This dish must be started at least the day before it is to be eaten, but it can be stored for several days in the refrigerator.

Ingredients

1.5 kg (3¼ lb) lean beef – blade steak, shin
2 calves' feet
200 g (7 oz) strips of lightly salted belly of pork, the size of a thumb
2 × 750 ml bottles red wine such as Côtes de Provence
3 very ripe tomatoes weighing 100 g (3½ oz) each
2 beef stock cubes
3 tablespoons chopped onion
8 small new carrots
2 large old carrots
24 small pickling or button onions
20 g (¾ oz) butter
5 crushed cloves of garlic
1 bouquet garni, composed of a bunch of parsley, a stick of celery, a large sprig of thyme, a bayleaf and a strip of orange peel
1 dessertspoon roughly crushed peppercorns
4 tablespoons capers preserved in vinegar
4 tablespoons chopped parsley
200 g (7 oz) flour

Recommended wines

light young red wines, for instance new Beaujolais Villages, Côtes de Provence, Graves

(continued on page 65)

Sea-Bass Fillets with Lettuce Leaves, Red Mullets,
Pierrot's Way, Salmon Escalopes Marinated with
Basil. (*Suprême de loup au vert de laitue, Les
petits rougets de mon ami Pierrot, Escalopes de
saumon frais en marinière*)

Saddle of Rabbit Salad, Nage of Freshwater
Crayfish Tails with Beurre Blanc. (*Salade de râble
de lapereau, Petite nage de queues d'écrevisses au
beurre blanc*)

Veal Medallion with Lemon, Fresh Fruit Sorbets.
Filets mignons de veau au citron,
Les sorbets framboise-citron-orange)

John Dory with Baby Vegetables
(*Blanc de Saint-Pierre à la crème de petits légumes*)

The day before (in the morning)

1 Cut the beef into pieces of about 60–70 g (2–2½ oz) each, and put them in a casserole. Add the chopped onions, the large carrots chopped, the bouquet garni, garlic and crushed peppercorns. Pour over the two bottles of wine. Mix well with a wooden spoon and leave to marinate for 4 hours in a cool place (but not in the refrigerator).

2 While the meat is marinating boil the calves' feet in 2 litres (3½ pints) unsalted water for 15 minutes.

3 Peel the little onions and the small carrots, and soften in the butter, with 4 tablespoons water and a pinch of salt, in a covered sauté pan for 20–25 minutes, then set them aside in a cool place. Remove the stalks from the tomatoes, cut them in two horizontally and press each half in the palm of your hand to squeeze out the seeds and moisture. Chop into coarse dice.

4 Bring the belly of pork strips, or lardons, to the boil in 2 litres (3½ pints) water. Boil for 2 minutes then drain and refresh in cold water.

5 After the meat has been marinating for 3½ hours, preheat the oven to 90°C/190°F/Mark ¼. Add to the meat in its marinade the calves' feet, lardons of belly of pork, tomatoes and stock cubes. Add cold water to cover the meat by 3 cm (1¼ inches) and cover the casserole. Seal the lid with a soft pliable paste made of 200 g (7 oz) flour and a little water, and cook in the slow oven for 5 hours.

6 After five hours, remove the casserole from the oven, loosen the seal of flour and water paste and take off the lid. Inhale the delicious aroma. Using a slotted spoon, carefully remove the chunks of beef and lardons of belly of pork and put them on one side in a deep dish. (This needs to be done exceedingly carefully, as the meat is very well-cooked and tends to disintegrate.) Remove the calves' feet and extract all their little bones. Cut the flesh into large dice and add to the meat and lardons. Tip the casserole on one side and remove as much as possible of the fat, which rises to the surface, with a spoon. Strain the sauce through a fine sieve *without*

(continued on page 66)

pressing it through with a spoon, which would cloud the liquid. Return to the heat and bring to the boil for a moment. Add a pinch of salt.

7 Choose a 3 litre (5¼ pint) terrine, and pour in an even layer of 5–6 tablespoons of the liquid. Sprinkle with half the capers and chopped parsley. Arrange a layer of half the beef, lardons and meat from the calves' feet and strew it with the cooked button onions (3). Lay the small carrots (3) on top lengthwise. Cover with a layer of sauce and sprinkle with the rest of the capers and parsley. Arrange the rest of the meat in a layer and pour over the rest of the sauce, which should just cover the beef. Put the terrine in the refrigerator for at least 8 hours, so that the sauce can set to a good jelly. If any sauce was left over, put it in a small dish in the refrigerator to set.

Serving the terrine
8 Run the hot tap briefly over the base of the terrine, then turn it out on a long serving-dish. If you have some jelly left over, cut it into cubes and strew them round the terrine. Serve accompanied by small pickled gherkins and a good green salad.

✷ I believe I have done justice to Tante Célestine's memory, and have not forgotten any of the ingredients she used. I watched her make this dish so often that I can remember it as if I could see her now.

Editor's note If calves' feet are difficult to obtain, 5 or 6 fresh pigs' trotters, chopped in half by the butcher, can be used instead. You will need an enormous pot to accommodate all these feet.

Rabbit in Jelly from the Moulin de Mougins

Gâteau de lapereau en gelée du Moulin

For three or four people

Reasonably simple
Moderately expensive
Preparation time: marination 12 hours
Cooking time: 2½ hours
Chilling time: 2¼ hours

Ingredients

1 young rabbit, skinned and gutted, weighing 2 kg (4½ lb), preferably a well-fed domestic rabbit.
200 g (7 oz) thin slices of lightly salt belly of pork without rind
200 ml (scant half-pint) dry white wine
500 ml (scant pint) aspic jelly made with 500 ml chicken stock **or** stock made with stock cubes and 4 leaves of gelatine or 4 level teaspoons of powdered gelatine
2 tablespoons chopped shallots
2 tablespoons chopped parsley
1 small clove of garlic chopped
1 generous sprig thyme
1 sprig rosemary
pepper

Recommended wines

a young and fruity wine, red, white or rosé – Côtes de Provence, Beaujolais, Chinon, Sancerre

✳ This is a reasonably simple dish to make and delightful to eat in the shade of an olive tree. (If you have no olive to hand, any tree will do. If you have no tree at all, close your eyes, imagine the sound of the cicadas and the Provençal sunshine, and if you have neither tree nor imagination, but love good food, simply eat this rabbit jelly and you will be happy....)

✳ If you include the saddle the pâté will serve four people; if not, three. The proportions of the other ingredients do not change.

One day in advance
1 Remove the heart, kidneys, liver and lungs of the rabbit. Cut off the feet and head and discard them. Remove the front legs by sliding a small sharp knife between the ribs and shoulder blades. Leave the hind legs on. Remove the saddle from the carcass – this is situated between the last rib and the top of the hind legs. If you are going to use it for a separate recipe (see saddle of rabbit salad, page 50) keep it whole; if not, and you prefer to use it in the rabbit jelly, cut it into two pieces along the backbone. Take the rib cage and cut off the neck. Carefully cut away the lower part of the ribs which is of no use to you (but may come in useful to your dog or cat). Cut the top part of the ribs into two pieces along the backbone. Now remove the two hind legs and cut each one in half.

2 Put the pieces in a large bowl with the white wine, shallots, garlic and all the herbs. Add pepper but do not add salt, as the salt in the salt pork and the jelly should be enough. Mix everything together thoroughly, press down in the marinade, cover, and leave in a cool place (but not in the refrigerator) for 12 hours.

Cooking the rabbit
3 Preheat the oven to 150°C/300°F/Mark 2. Carefully line the terrine with thin slices of salt belly of pork, overlapping as little as possible. Put in the pieces of rabbit and press them well down. Pour over the marinade and then cover completely with half the melted aspic. Place the terrine in a bain-marie filled with enough water to come half-way up the sides and bring to the boil on top of the stove. Cover the pâté with a sheet of kitchen foil, shiny side down, and cook in the oven for 2 hours.

4 Take the rabbit out of the oven, pour the rest of the melted aspic into the terrine and allow to chill in the refrigerator for 2½ hours. Turn out on to a chilled plate and serve with a green salad and black olives.

✳ If you have time, it is best to cook the rabbit in jelly the day before you want to serve it, so that you can be absolutely sure that the jelly sets firmly. It will keep in the refrigerator for 2–3 days.

Fine Chicken Liver Pâté
Pâté fin de foie de volaille

For six people	Fairly simple
	Inexpensive
	Preparation time: 30 minutes
	Cooking time: 5 minutes
	To be made the day before it is needed
Ingredients	12 large chicken livers
	1 tablespoon finely-chopped parsley
	3 tablespoons finely-chopped onion (new for preference)
	a pinch of thyme
	2 tablespoons olive oil
	200 g (7 oz) fresh white breadcrumbs
	250 ml (scant half-pint) cold milk
	1 egg yolk
	salt, pepper
Recommended wines	White Sancerre or Côtes du Rhône

✷ This is a delicious cold first course, eaten with a mixed salad seasoned with olive oil and wine vinegar. Spread the pâté lavishly on large slices of toasted pain de campagne, and you will discover how good life can be. . . .

The day before

1 Two or three hours before you are ready to make the pâté, clean the livers, removing the little veins and membranes and cutting away all yellow or greenish traces of the gall bladder, which will give a bitter flavour. Put the livers in a bowl and cover with all but 4 tablespoons of the cold milk. Soak for 2–3 hours, then drain the livers and dry with kitchen paper. Season them with salt and pepper. Discard the milk.

2 Heat 2 tablespoons of olive oil in a frying-pan, and when it begins to smoke add the livers and cook them rapidly, turning constantly with a wooden spatula so they brown all over. Remove them with a slotted spoon and put them in a colander to drain. Cook the chopped onions in the oil remaining in the frying-pan until they begin to turn golden, which will take about 10 minutes. Meanwhile soak the bread in the remaining 4 tablespoons of milk in a bowl.

Assembling the pâté

3 Drain the bread and squeeze it between your hands to remove the moisture. Pass it and the livers through the fine blade of a mincer or chop briefly in a food-processor, and place in a large shallow sauté pan. Using a wooden spoon, mix in the cooked onion, chopped parsley, thyme and egg yolk. Cook over a gentle heat for 5 minutes, stirring constantly with a wooden spoon, and allow the mixture to come to the boil very briefly. If it seems too dry, and likely to stick, moisten the mixture with 2 tablespoons of milk. Season with salt and pepper and turn the mixture into a terrine, pressing it down well. Cover with a rectangle of grease-proof paper rubbed with olive oil. Leave in a cool place or in the refrigerator for 24 hours.

Editor's note If your chicken livers are on the small side use more, or cut down on the number of breadcrumbs.

Egg Dishes

Swiss Chard Omelette
Trucca cannoise ou trouchia

For two people	Relatively simple *Preparation time:* 1 hour
Ingredients	800 g (1 lb 12 oz) tender Swiss chard or blettes 4 eggs 160 g (5½ oz) onion, cut into fine rounds 5 tablespoons olive oil 2 tablespoons grated Parmesan cheese half a clove of garlic 1 tablespoon fine dried breadcrumbs a pinch of thyme flowers 6 chopped basil leaves (optional) 1 tablespoon chopped parsley salt, pepper
Recommended wines	Fresh young dry white or rosé wines (Côtes de Provence)

1 Remove the green part of the chard leaves, keeping the white ribs for another meal. Wash the leaves in three lots of water and drain them well. Cut them roughly into ribbons with scissors.

2 Put the finely-sliced onion in a medium saucepan with 2 table-spoons olive oil, and allow to cook for 5 minutes. Add the chard and cook gently for about 20 minutes until the moisture contained in the leaves has evaporated completely. Season with salt and pepper.

3 Break the eggs into a large bowl and add the Parmesan cheese, thyme, parsley, basil and the half clove of garlic scored with the prongs of a fork. Season with salt and pepper and beat everything together thoroughly with a fork.

4 Drain the oil from the chard and onions and add them to the beaten eggs in the bowl. Mix them together thoroughly and taste for seasoning. Put the remaining 3 tablespoons of olive oil in a frying-pan and heat gently. When a blue haze rises, pour in the egg mixture. Stir once with a fork, then leave to cook undisturbed until the upper part is just beginning to set. Sprinkle with the bread-crumbs and turn the omelette over. (The simplest way of doing this is to hold a flat plate over the frying-pan, turn it upside down and then slide the up-turned omelette back in the pan.) Cook for a further 2–3 minutes to brown the breadcrumbs, turn the omelette over again on to a plate and serve with the breadcrumbed side up.

✳ The Trucca can be served cold, sprinkled with olive oil and served with small black olives.

✳ It is very important to cook this omelette very gently. It can also be cooked in a very low oven.

Harlequin Omelette
Omelette arlequin

For four to six people	Fairly simple *Preparation time:* $2\frac{1}{4}$ hours
Ingredients	9 eggs 400 g (14 oz) very ripe tomatoes 500 g (18 oz) fresh spinach 75 g ($2\frac{1}{2}$ oz) grated Gruyère cheese 2 cloves of garlic a pinch of thyme flowers 8 tablespoons whipping cream 8 tablespoons olive oil nutmeg salt, pepper
Recommended wines	Dry white wines (white Graves, Saint-Véran, blanc de Cassis)
Equipment	A pâté dish or terrine 20 cm (8 inches) long or a round ovenproof cocotte or soufflé dish 20 cm (8 inches) across and at least 12 cm (5 inches) deep. A bain-marie

1 Preheat the oven to 120°C/250°F/Mark ½. Pick over the spinach and wash it thoroughly, changing the water three times. Drain it carefully. Plunge the tomatoes into boiling water for 2 seconds, then refresh under cold running water. Peel them, cut them in half and squeeze them to expel the seeds and juice. Chop them coarsely into dice. Peel the two cloves of garlic.

2 Heat 2 tablespoons of olive oil in a medium-sized saucepan until a blue haze rises. Add the chopped tomato together with the thyme and a pinch of salt and allow to cook until the moisture from the tomatoes has evaporated completely. Put 3 tablespoons of olive oil into a larger saucepan and heat until a blue haze rises, then add the spinach, the garlic and a pinch of salt. Stir with a wooden spoon and cook until the moisture has completely evaporated. When the tomatoes and spinach are cooked put them on 2 separate plates, remove the garlic from the spinach and allow to cool.

3 Get out 3 bowls and break three eggs into each. Add the spinach, 3 tablespoons cream, a grating of nutmeg and salt and pepper to the eggs in the first bowl and whisk everything together. Add the tomatoes, 2 tablespoons cream and salt and pepper to the eggs in the second bowl and whisk. Add the grated gruyère, 3 tablespoons cream and salt and pepper to the eggs in the third bowl and whisk.

4 Oil the inside of the terrine or other dish lavishly and pour in the tomato mixture. Stand the dish in a bain-marie half-filled with hot water and cook in the preheated oven for 15 minutes. Then, very gently, pour in the cheese mixture and return to the oven for a further 15 minutes. Finally pour in the spinach mixture and cook for 20 minutes more. When the omelette is cooked let it rest for 10–15 minutes in a warm place before turning it out on to a dish. Serve hot, cutting it into slices or wedges according to the shape of the dish it was cooked in.

✳ This omelette can also be served cold, as a first course, with a little olive oil sprinkled on each slice.

Tomato and Basil Omelette

Omelette à la tomate fraîche et aux feuilles de basilic

For two people Simple
Inexpensive
Preparation time: 20 minutes

Ingredients 6 fresh eggs
4 large ripe tomatoes, each about the size of a tennis ball
4 tablespoons olive oil
10 leaves of fresh basil
4 sprigs parsley
1 sprig thyme
1 bayleaf
1 clove of garlic
salt, pepper

Recommended wines Rosé or white (Coteaux de Nice or any other fresh-tasting wine)

1 Remove the stalks and cores of the tomatoes with a small sharp knife and plunge them into boiling water for 2 seconds. Refresh under cold running water and remove the skin. Cut each in half and squeeze in your hand to press out seeds and juice. Chop into coarse dice and put them in a saucepan with the bayleaf and 2 tablespoons of olive oil. Allow to cook over a brisk heat for 15 minutes until all the moisture has evaporated.

2 Put the coarsely-chopped basil and parsley in a bowl together with the leaves from the sprig of thyme and add the clove of garlic scored with the prongs of a fork. Break in the eggs, add salt and pepper and beat with a fork. Add the cooked tomato dice and mix well.

3 Put 2 tablespoons of olive oil in a frying-pan and put over a brisk heat. When a blue haze rises pour in the egg mixture and cook, stirring continuously with a fork in a circular motion. Stop stirring when the eggs have set evenly, but are still creamy, and leave over the heat for a minute to brown the bottom of the omelette. Put a plate over the top of the pan, remove from the heat and turn upside down. Lift the pan to reveal a delicious golden omelette which you can eat hot, warm, or cold with a few small black Nice olives.

Editor's note Provençal tomatoes are less watery than the more northerly varieties which therefore take longer to evaporate to a reasonably thick consistency – allow about 20–30 minutes.

Courgette Omelette
Omelette aux rouelles de courgettes

For two people	Simple
	Inexpensive
	Preparation time: 30 minutes

Ingredients	300 g (10½ oz) small slender courgettes, very firm and smooth
	5 eggs
	6 tablespoons olive oil
	1 teaspoon chopped fresh basil
	1 tablespoon chopped parsley
	salt, pepper

Recommended wines	Dry white or rosé wines (Provence or Côtes du Rhône)

1 Wipe the courgettes with a cloth and trim both ends. Do not peel them. Cut into very fine rounds. Heat 4 tablespoons of olive oil in a frying-pan over a brisk heat until a blue haze rises. Add the courgettes and stir over a brisk heat, until they are almost cooked but still firm. Drain them in a colander.

2 Break the eggs into a bowl, season with salt and pepper, and add the chopped basil and parsley. Beat thoroughly with a fork.

3 Clean the frying-pan and put in 2 tablespoons of olive oil. Heat gently, add the drained courgettes, salt lightly and let them heat through. Pour in the beaten eggs and cook, stirring all the time in a circular motion with a fork. When the omelette is done, place a plate over the pan and quickly turn it upside down, holding the plate with the other hand so that the omelette drops neatly on to the plate golden-brown side upwards. Serve hot, warm, or cold sprinkled with olive oil and accompanied by a few small black Nice olives. Provence on a plate!

Scrambled Eggs with Anchovies
Oeufs brouillés aux filets d'anchois

For two people	Simple
	Inexpensive
	Preparation time: 20 minutes

Ingredients	6 eggs
	10 anchovy fillets in olive oil
	12 stoned green olives
	2 slices white bread
	50 g (1¾ oz) butter
	salt, pepper

Recommended wines	Dry white wines (Côtes de Provence or Côtes du Rhône)

1 Break the eggs into a bowl and beat them with a fork. Do not add salt. Put two plates to heat. Plunge the olives into boiling water in a small saucepan and when it returns to the boil remove the pan from the heat. Slice six of the anchovy fillets in half lengthwise and put them on a small plate, being careful not to crush them.

2 Heat half the butter in a small saucepan. Add the four whole anchovy fillets and stir gently till they have dissolved. Add the beaten eggs and cook, stirring all the time, until they are set but still creamy. Remove the pan from the heat and season carefully with salt and pepper. Stir in the rest of the butter cut in small pieces, using a wooden spatula.

3 Divide the scrambled eggs between the two hot plates and decorate with strips of anchovy (1). Drain the olives and arrange on top in a star. Toast the slices of bread, cut each into four 'strips' and 'frame' the scrambled eggs with them.

Fried Eggs with Wine Vinegar
Oeufs au plat avec la giclée de vinaigre de vin

For two people	Simple Inexpensive
Ingredients	4 large brown eggs (6 if you enjoy them as much as I do) 30 g (1 oz) butter 4 tablespoons good wine vinegar salt, pepper
Recommended wines	A simple white or red wine, fresh-tasting and fruity

1 Rub a 15 cm (6-inch) frying-pan with 4 tablespoons of fine salt and wipe thoroughly to eliminate every grain.

2 Break 2 or 3 eggs, according to your appetite, into a bowl, taking care not to break the yolks. Heat the butter in the frying-pan, and when it turns golden, slip in the eggs very carefully. Cook, puncturing any air bubbles which form in the egg whites with a fork. Don't worry if the eggs go crisp and golden round the edge. When they are cooked the way you like them, season with salt and freshly-ground pepper and slide on to a heated plate. Pour 2 tablespoons of wine vinegar into the pan. Allow to reduce by half and pour over the eggs.

3 Wipe out the pan with a cloth or kitchen-paper and repeat the process with the remaining eggs.

✳ This is a controversial recipe. Some people swear that the butter should not be allowed to colour; others cook the whites first on their own and then slide the yolks on top (having first salted the whites to prevent the yolks from being marked). Each way has its point, but in this book I have given the recipe I make for myself and my friends. Fried eggs cooked in this way are, incidentally, among the most irresistible of all dishes. Many is the time that I have suddenly had a longing for three fried eggs – usually after midnight, when I am among friends, and guests who have finished dinner and are mulling away the evening with a liqueur. The sight of the eggs cooking is too much for them all, and they always end up by joining me. I know few dishes so powerful!

It is perfectly true that one judges a cook by his or her sauces; the sauce reveals the man, the poet, the artist – in other words, the cook. Each sauce has its day and expresses the spirit and humour of the moment. The smallest thing – a passing whim, the memory of a flower or of a lover, the bouquet of a wine, the aroma of a fruit, a truffle or a herb can alter the most rigid recipe. And, finally, only happy cooks make good sauces.

So, here are some sauces. Never mind the 'great sauces', they don't really matter all that much. What is important, surely, is that your sauces should add character and wit to steaks and escalopes, chicken and fish?

Sauces

Sauce Grelette
Sauce grelette à la tomate fraîche

For four   Simple
people   Inexpensive
Preparation time: 1 hour

Ingredients   3 handsome ripe tomatoes weighing about
100 g (3½ oz) each
3 tablespoons double cream
2 tablespoons wine vinegar
1 teaspoon strong Dijon mustard
10 finely-chopped leaves of tarragon – preferably fresh, but you can substitute 15 tarragon leaves preserved in white wine or
vinegar
1 tablespoon finely-chopped parsley
1 teaspoon finely-chopped chervil
1 teaspoon cognac
salt, cayenne pepper **or** tabasco

Uses   With cold fish, lobsters and other crustaceans,
salads or vegetables.

1 Wipe the tomatoes and remove the stalks. Plunge them in boiling water for 2 seconds and refresh under cold running water: the skin can now be removed without difficulty. Cut each in half horizontally (that is, with the stalk side facing downwards). Press the halves in your hand to squeeze out seeds and juice. Take one of the tomatoes (two halves) and cut into 1 cm ($\frac{1}{2}$ inch) cubes. Salt lightly to extract still more moisture and set aside in a sieve. Chop the other tomatoes to a fine purée, salt them and put to drain in a fine-meshed sieve.

2 Pour the cream into a bowl and add the mustard, wine vinegar, cognac, salt and a pinch of cayenne pepper (enough to cover the tip of a knife). You can replace the cayenne with 2 or 3 drops of tabasco. Whisk until the cream thickens, but do not let it separate. Add the purée of tomatoes (don't add the diced tomatoes yet), and the chopped parsley, tarragon and chervil. Whisk thoroughly, then fold in the diced tomatoes with a wooden spatula. Add salt if necessary. Keep in a cold place and serve in a sauceboat.

✳ It was twenty years ago, when I was trying to find a sauce to go with a pâté of sole en croûte, that I discovered this fresh-tasting, unassertive mixture of ingredients. Next I had to find a name for it. It was very slightly tart – *aigrelette* – so why not *Sauce aigrelette*? But that wasn't exactly right for such a delicate sauce, so I simply shortened the word to 'slender' – *grelette* – and that's how *Sauce grelette* came about.

Créosa Sauce

Sauce creosa

It is difficult to make this particular sauce for
fewer than eight to ten people, but it keeps
well for several days and even improves
with keeping.
Simple
Inexpensive
Preparation time: 45 minutes, **24 hours in
advance**

Ingredients 1 onion weighing about 150 g (5½ oz)
3 tomatoes weighing about 400 g (14 oz) altogether
1 small cucumber weighing about 200 g (7 oz)
1 sweet red pepper weighing about 150 g (5½ oz)
100 g (3½ oz) pickled gherkins
100 g (3½ oz) pickled capers
1 teaspoon chopped tarragon
50 g (1¾ oz) chopped parsley
200 ml (⅓ pint) olive oil (13 tablespoons)
3 generous tablespoons wine vinegar
4 tablespoons Dijon mustard
salt, pepper

1 Peel the onion and the cucumber. Cut the latter in half length-ways and remove the seeds with a teaspoon. Remove the stalks from the pepper and shake out any remaining seeds. Remove the stalks from the tomatoes, cut them in half and press to squeeze out the seeds and juice.

2 Cut all the vegetables into small dice the size of very small peas and place in a stoneware or porcelain bowl. Add the gherkins cut into pea-sized dice, together with the capers, the chopped tarragon and parsley, the mustard, the olive oil and the wine vinegar. Season generously with salt and pepper. Mix very thoroughly with a wooden spatula, cover the bowl and keep in a cold place (but **not** in the refrigerator) for 24 hours before serving.

✳ This is an excellent sauce which is served – almost like a salad – with grilled or roasted beef and with all kinds of barbecued foods, including fish.

✳ I found this sauce in South America, where it appears on every table, though in a much simpler version. This usually consists of diced tomato, onion and pepper in wine vinegar and is often very hot.

Watercress Sauce
Sauce cressonette

For six people   Fairly simple
Inexpensive
Preparation time: 10 minutes

Ingredients   2 bunches of watercress
Juice of 1 lemon
8 generous tablespoons whipping cream
1 egg yolk
1 teaspoon strong mustard
200 ml ($\frac{1}{3}$ pint) olive oil
salt, cayenne pepper

Uses   Cold veal and chicken, fish, lobsters and other
crustaceans, hot or cold boiled or steamed
vegetables.

✱ This light and fragrant sauce goes perfectly with a summer dish such as a cold (but not chilled) roast or poached chicken served with cold poached vegetables – haricots verts, small new potatoes, courgettes and so on. It is equally delicious with fish served cold or warm.

✱ I could write a whole chapter on the ludicrous illusions and superstitions which many people have about mayonnaise – 'You *must* always use a wooden spoon', 'Don't breathe into the bowl', 'Always whisk in the same direction', 'In summer you must always make it in the cellar or some other cool place' and even – 'certain phases of the moon are unfavourable to mayonnaise'. Can the sauce *really* be so capricious? What nonsense! Nothing is easier than mayonnaise, provided you follow my two simple rules.

Preparing the watercress
1 Bring 1 litre (1¾ pints) of well salted water to the boil and plunge in the well-washed watercress for 10 seconds. Refresh under cold running water and drain. Remove fifty or so leaves and set on one side in a bowl of cold water. Press the remaining watercress between your hands to extract the water and purée in a liquidiser or through the fine blade of a mouli-légumes. If you use a liquidiser the purée may be a bit dry, in which case moisten it with 3–4 table-spoons of olive oil. If the watercress is at all fibrous strain the purée through a fine sieve. Keep in a cool place.

Preparing the mayonnaise
2 To make a successful mayonnaise you need only remember two pieces of advice: none of the ingredients, not even the bowl in which it is made, should be chilled. If you have added the oil too fast you can rescue it by adding a dessertspoon of lukewarm water and whisking rather fast. So, to make mayonnaise all you have to do is put the egg yolk, the mustard, the juice of half a lemon and a little salt in a bowl. Mix them well and forget them for 5 minutes. Then add the oil in a thin stream, whisking all the time until all the oil is incorporated. Add the rest of the lemon juice. That's all.

3 Add the watercress purée to the mayonnaise.

4 Put the cream in another bowl and whisk until thick. Season with salt. Mix the cream and the watercress mayonnaise together. Drain the whole watercress leaves (1) and dry them on a towel or kitchen-paper. Fold them into the mayonnaise and cream mixture. Add a pinch of cayenne pepper and keep the sauce in a cool place. Serve in a sauceboat.

Vinaigrette Dressings

Vinaigrettes are usually oil-based – olive, walnut, arachide (ground-nut) sunflower, colza, corn, grape-pip, soybean, cotton-seed, sesame-seed and poppy-seed oils can all be used. Then there are the vinegars – cider, wine, sherry, honey, pineapple and other fruits such as raspberry, cherry and gooseberry. (Unfortunately, there are also the distilled vinegars, low on taste and strong on acidity.) Lemon or lime juice, verjus or mustard can all be used instead of vinegar to add the necessary acidity.

Herbs play an important part in salads too – chervil, parsley, chives, tarragon, celery, garlic, onion and chilli peppers. Finally, we must not forget salt and pepper.

All these ingredients 'marry' with each other in varying ways which go particularly well with one salad or another. Choosing the right dressing is obviously a matter of taste, but in any case consider the type of salad – a tender salad deserves a delicately flavoured dressing, while tougher salads can stand a stronger dressing.

Wine should not be drunk with salads because the acidity of the dressing ruins the flavour of the wine irreparably.

Editor's note

Olive oil is the finest oil known to man. It is a naturally delicious oil that needs no refining. It has a lovely flavour, particularly in salad dressing. Try and find pure virgin oil which is obtained from the first pressing of the olives and extracted without heat. Provençal olive oil – full and fruity – is made from green (unripe) olives.

Refined or second-grade olive oil is extracted under heat, by pressure. It is more or less colourless, and doesn't have the same pure flavour as virgin olive oil.

Walnut oil with its delicious strong nutty flavour is only used cold as it doesn't stand up well to heat. It is wonderful on robust farm salads, but unfortunately does not keep well.

Oil of arachide, peanut oil is the French chef's favourite cooking oil. Buy a good quality oil of arachide and use it both on salads, when the flavour is mild and sweet, and for cooking.

Sunflower oil Mild and with a thin texture, this oil is used on its own where a very light dressing is needed, or blended with olive oil for a dressing with a slight olive flavour.

Rape-seed or colza oil This oil is one of the cheapest to produce, but is usually used in blended oils, since it has the reputation of being carcinogenic. Blended oils are not really quite good enough to use raw in salad dressing and are used in general as frying oils.

Corn oil is not one of the best oils for making salad dressings, being somewhat bland and viscous.

Soybean oil is a not unpleasant, although somewhat viscous, oil for salad dressing.

Cotton-seed oil has a pronounced flavour very much liked in Egypt and some parts of the Middle East. It is somewhat heavy in texture and often deep golden in colour.

Sesame-seed oil is a good light oil with a pleasant nutty flavour. It has very good keeping qualities.

Verjus or verjuice is an acid juice made from unripe grapes. It is used in the making of several kinds of mustard. You can make it by pressing unripe grapes or gooseberries to extract their juice. Verjuice was used a great deal in cooking in medieval times, and is sharp, like lemon juice (which can be used instead).

Wine vinegar Ordinary French wine vinegar is seldom as strong as the wine vinegar exported to other countries. To overcome the difference either use less vinegar or dilute it half and half with wine of the same colour or with water.

✱ If you eat salad every day, you can well make a large quantity of vinaigrette all at once. 1 litre (1¾ pints) of oil will make enough for about twenty-five salads. Make the vinaigrette in a large bowl and then put it in a bottle, which only needs a shake before dressing the salad. Herbs should only be added to the required quantity of dressing just before you dress the salad.

Traditional Vinaigrette
La vinaigrette traditionelle

For two or Simple
three people Inexpensive (depending on the oil you use)
Preparation time: 5–10 minutes

Plain vinaigrette
Use 4 tablespoons oil to 1 tablespoon vinegar. Salt and pepper. The vinegar can be replaced by lemon juice.

Vinaigrette with mustard
Use 1 teaspoon strong Dijon mustard to 5 tablespoons oil and 1 tablespoon vinegar. Salt and pepper.

Vinaigrette with herbs
Make either of the vinaigrettes given above and add chopped chervil, tarragon, chives, parsley, basil, shallots, onions or garlic.

Vinaigrette with Creamed Garlic
Vinaigrette à la crème d'ail

For two people Simple
Inexpensive

Ingredients 2 cloves of garlic peeled and crushed
$\frac{1}{2}$ teaspoon strong Dijon mustard
1 teaspoon wine vinegar
2 tablespoons double cream
1 tablespoon olive oil

Uses With curly endive (chicorée frisée) cos lettuce (romaine) Batavian endive (scarole). (See page 46 for notes on the different salads.)

Mix all the ingredients in a bowl with a whisk. Season with a pinch of salt and a little pepper.

Pernod Sauce

Sauce à la crème d'anis

For four people	Simple Fairly inexpensive *Preparation time:* 30 minutes cooking, 15 minutes finishing
Ingredients	1 fennel bulb weighing 100 g (3½ oz) 2 hard-boiled eggs 1 teaspoon Dijon mustard juice of 1 lemon 5 tablespoons olive oil 4 tablespoons well chilled whipping cream 1 teaspoon Pernod **or** other pastis salt, pepper
Uses	With fish and shellfish served hot or cold

1 Trim and quarter the fennel and cook it in boiling salted water for about 30 minutes. When it is cooked, squeeze the pieces in a tea towel to extract the water.

2 Sieve the two hard-boiled egg yolks and the fennel into a large bowl with a mouli-légumes. Purée it thoroughly and scrape any bits which have stuck to the blade into the bowl. Add the mustard, lemon juice, salt and 2–3 turns of the peppermill to this purée. Whisk thoroughly and then whisk in the olive oil slowly as if you were making mayonnaise.

3 Put the cream together with the Pernod in a smaller bowl, and whisk until the cream thickens, then fold the cream into the fennel mixture in the large bowl. Taste the mixture and add salt, pepper and, if you like, a little more lemon juice.

✳ This is a pleasant sauce, redolent of the Midi.

Roquefort Sauce
Sauce au Roquefort

Version I – for delicate salads

Ingredients   40 g (1½ oz) Roquefort cheese
1 tablespoon wine vinegar
5 tablespoons whipping cream
1 tablespoon chopped chives

Put the cheese on a plate and crush it with a fork. Put the crumbs into a bowl and whisk in the vinegar, the cream and finally the chives. Add salt if necessary – Roquefort is already rather salty – and pepper.

Version II – for more robust salads

Ingredients   40 g (1½ oz) Roquefort cheese
½ teaspoon strong Dijon mustard
1 tablespoon wine vinegar
4 tablespoons walnut oil

Put the cheese on a plate and crush it with a fork. Put the cheese crumbs into a bowl and whisk in the mustard, the wine vinegar and finally the walnut oil. Season with salt (depending on how salty the cheese and mustard are) and pepper.

✳ I have given two versions of this sauce, the first for sweet, delicate salads such as lettuce, lamb's lettuce (màche), chicory, celery and cos lettuce, and the second for more robust salads – curly endive, Batavia, cornette, (barbe-de-capucin). (Descriptions of these and other salad plants appear at the beginning of the chapter on First Courses.)

✳ If possible, persuade your grocer or cheese-merchant to sell you the crumbs of Roquefort which collect when this delicious crumbly cheese is cut. It will be less expensive and all from the middle of the cheese, which is the best part.

Melted Butter

Beurre Fondu

For two people Very easy
Cheap
Preparation time: 5 minutes

Ingredients 100 g (3½ oz) very fresh unsalted butter, cut in
pieces
salt
juice of half a lemon (optional)

Uses With fish, with poached, roasted or grilled
shellfish, or with artichokes, asparagus,
leeks, broccoli, etc.

Bring 5 tablespoons of water to the boil in a small saucepan, together with a pinch of salt. Add half the butter, in pieces, and allow to come to a galloping boil. Remove from the heat and gradually whisk in the rest of the butter, a few pieces at a time. If you like, the juice of half a lemon can be added at this point. Serve in a sauceboat.

Beurre Blanc

For two people Simplicity itself (this is heresy)
Fairly inexpensive
Preparation time: 10 minutes

Ingredients 80 g (2¾ oz) chilled unsalted butter, cut in little
    dice
3 tablespoons white wine vinegar
5 tablespoons dry white wine
1 tablespoon double cream
1 teaspoon chopped shallot
salt, pepper

Uses Beurre Blanc is a delicate companion for
poached fish and shellfish, asparagus, artichokes, leeks, lambs' or calves' brains – in
fact for most things cooked in water or
court-bouillon.

Recommended Young dry white wines, not too fruity.
wines

1 Put the vinegar, white wine and chopped shallot in a small saucepan with sloping sides and reduce over a moderate heat until you have barely 2 tablespoons of liquid left.

2 Add the cream; when it starts to boil, which will be almost immediately, turn the heat very, very low and whisk in the diced butter until the butter is completely incorporated in the sauce. Season with salt and pepper, strain and serve hot in a sauceboat.

Now tell me what is so difficult about that? – perhaps the main problem lies in the endless complications, all quite pointless, which most recipes inflict on us.

✸ If you need to prepare this sauce in advance, it can be reheated very gently, whisking all the time. But as a general rule Beurre Blanc should be served as soon as it is ready.

✸ Here we have one of the prime subjects of argument and controversy. For years this poor sauce has been written off as being only for the great experts. So much so that scarcely a single cookery book dares to tackle it, for fear of bringing down indignant protests. There are probably one hundred recipes for it, all of which arrive at almost the same result, each one claiming to be the one and only original version. So I am offering one more 'original' recipe (which many people, in fact, may think is heresy). But at least this version has the advantage of being simple and I must say that I find it very good. You must decide about that for yourself.

Fresh Hot Tomato Sauce
Coulis frais de tomate

For two people   Very simple
Inexpensive
Preparation time: 15–20 minutes

Ingredients   4 ripe tomatoes weighing 70–80 g (2½–2¾ oz)
each
1 medium onion
1 clove of garlic, peeled
1 small bouquet garni, made up of a sprig of
thyme, a bayleaf, a small piece of celery, and
4 sprigs of parsley tied up with a thread
½ teaspoon sugar
2 tablespoons unsalted butter
salt, pepper

Uses   With baked fish, pasta, rice, poached vegetables (such as cauliflower, courgettes, fennel,
haricot beans), poached lambs' or calves'
brains, and even with sautéd veal escalopes
or chops.

1 Peel the onion and slice it in thin rounds. Put them in a saucepan together with 2 tablespoons of butter and 2 tablespoons of water. Allow to soften without browning, stirring occasionally with a wooden spoon. This will take about 5 minutes.

2 Remove the stalks from the tomatoes, wipe them and cut them in half horizontally. Press each half in your hand to expel seeds and excess moisture, then cut each half into four. Add to the onions which have been softening and wilting for a good 5 minutes, together with the peeled clove of garlic, bouquet garni, sugar and a tiny pinch of salt. Cook for 10 minutes, stirring all the time. At certain times of the year tomatoes can be somewhat dry, so you may have to add 3–4 tablespoons of water.

3 Remove the bouquet garni and purée the sauce in a liquidiser (or sieve through the fine blade of a mouli-légumes). Season with salt and pepper, reheat and serve.

✳ And if you like the flavours of Provençe, add some finely-shredded basil leaves and 2 tablespoons of olive oil. A real treat!

'Marchand de Vin' Sauce
Sauce marchand de vin

For two people	Very simple Inexpensive *Preparation time:* 5 minutes

Ingredients	5 tablespoons of the wine which you have chosen to drink with the meal 60 g (2 oz) butter ½ teaspoon Dijon mustard 2 tablespoons finely-chopped onion 1 clove of garlic, crushed 1 sprig thyme salt, pepper

Recommended wines	Red Beaujolais – Fleurie, Juliénas, Brouilly (not to be confused with Beaujolais Villages or Beaujolais Primeur).

1 Having cooked your steak take it out of the frying-pan and keep it hot. Throw away the fat, but on no account wash the frying-pan, which will be encrusted with delicious caramelised juices.

2 Put in the chopped onion and a teaspoon of butter and allow to cook fast for 2 minutes, then pour in the wine and add the garlic and thyme. Boil rapidly until only 3–4 tablespoons of liquid are left.

3 Remove the pan from the heat and whisk in the rest of the butter, cut into little pieces, add the mustard. Season with pepper (in theory the sauce should already be salty enough). Add the pink juices which have run out of the meat.

4 Arrange the pieces of meat on hot plates and strain the sauce over them.

✳ This is a grand sauce made from simple ingredients.

Shallot Sauce
Sauce échalote

For two people	Very simple
	Inexpensive
	Preparation time: 10 minutes
	Finishing: 5 minutes

Ingredients	60 g (2 oz) unsalted butter
	80 g (2¾ oz) finely-chopped shallots
	A small bunch of parsley, chopped
	4 tablespoons wine vinegar
	salt, pepper

Recommended wines	Red Beaujolais, young Burgundy such as Volnay

1 Having cooked your steak, take it out of the pan and keep it hot. Throw away the fat without washing the pan. Melt the butter in the same pan. Soften the chopped shallots in the butter, allowing them to cook for about 2 minutes.

2 Pour in the vinegar and allow to reduce by half. Season with salt and pepper and add the chopped parsley and the blood which has run out of the meat.

3 Arrange the steaks on hot plates and cover them with the shallot sauce.

✳ I like serving this sauce with skirt steak. Incidentally, it isn't expensive cuts such as fillet and rumpsteak which appeal to the expert, but those excellent juicy cuts which butchers and chefs like to keep for their own enjoyment.

This sauce, and the two which follow, are for serving with steaks cooked in a frying-pan – rumpsteak, rib steak, sirloin (entrecôte) steak or skirt. They must all be made in the frying-pan in which the meat was cooked.

Anchovy Sauce
Sauce fondue d'anchois

For two people   Very simple
Inexpensive
Preparation time: 5 minutes

Ingredients   60 g (2 oz) unsalted butter
4 anchovy fillets preserved in oil
juice of ½ lemon
2 tablespoons chopped parsley
pepper

Recommended   Provençal or Côtes du Rhône red wines
wines

1 Having cooked your steak, take it out of the frying-pan and keep it hot. Throw away the fat without washing the pan.

2 Put the anchovies and the butter in the same pan and let them melt, crushing them with a fork. Keep the pan over the heat and stir in the lemon juice, parsley and a turn of the peppermill. Add the juices from the steaks.

3 Arrange the steaks on hot plates and cover them with the sauce.

✸ You can serve this summery dish with a mixed green salad. I enjoy it most with a slice of rare steak sandwiched between two slices of French bread lightly toasted on one side and sprinkled with the sauce. I don't know which is better, the bread or the meat!

✸ Do not put much salt on the meat if you are serving this sauce.

Fish, Crustaceans and Shellfish

Nage of Freshwater Crayfish Tails with Beurre Blanc

Petite nage de queues d'écrevisses au beurre blanc

For two people	Fairly simple
	Expensive
	Preparation time: 1¼ hours
	Finishing time: 5 minutes

Ingredients

1 kg (2¼ lb) live freshwater crayfish **or** Dublin Bay prawns

1 medium carrot ⎫
1 white part of a leek ⎪ cleaned, peeled and
1 stick celery ⎬ finely sliced for
4 shallots ⎪ the nage or court-
1 onion ⎭ bouillon

120 g (4½ oz) butter
2 shallots (for the beurre blanc)
500 ml (scant pint) dry white wine
3 tablespoons white wine vinegar

2 sprigs parsley ⎫ with stalks
1 small bunch of chervil ⎬ removed
8 tarragon leaves ⎭

a muslin bag, carefully tied up with a thread, containing: ½ bayleaf, a stalk of diced fennel, 10 white peppercorns and a sprig of thyme (fresh if possible)
coarse salt, pepper

Preparing the nage and the crayfish
1 Put the thinly-sliced carrot, leek, celery, shallots and onion in a saucepan with 1 teaspoon butter and 4 tablespoons water. Salt lightly, and cook over a very low heat, covered, for 20 minutes. (This slow cooking process is known as *étuver*.) Then add 400 ml (scant ¾ pint) white wine and the little bag of herbs and spices, and simmer for 15–20 minutes. Watch the seasoning and the cooking time very carefully, as the vegetables should keep a trace of 'bite' to their texture. Remove the little parcel of herbs.

2 While the vegetables are cooking, bring 4 litres (7 pints) of water, seasoned with 2 tablespoons of coarse salt, to the boil and plunge in the crayfish. When the water has come back to the boil, cook for 4 minutes. Then lift out the crayfish with a slotted spoon and drain them in a colander. When they have cooled slightly, detach the tails and shell them by pinching the carapace between your thumb and forefinger. Keep the flesh, together with two of the head-shells, on one side.

Preparing the beurre blanc
3 Take a small saucepan with sloping sides and put into it two coarsely-chopped shallots, the remaining white wine and 3 tablespoons wine vinegar. Reduce over a brisk heat watching attentively until only 2 tablespoons of liquid are left. If you find you have overdone the reduction, stretch it with a little of the nage (1). Remove the pan from the heat and, little by little, incorporate 110 g (scant 4 oz) butter, cut into large dice, whisking vigorously, until you have a sauce the consistency of cream. Season with salt and pepper. If the sauce curdles, because you have overdone the heat or added the butter too quickly, you can put two tablespoons of the nage (1) into another saucepan and pour the curdled sauce in to it in a trickle, whisking all the time. You can keep the sauce hot by putting a folded newspaper in the bottom of a large saucepan, placing the pan containing the beurre blanc on top of the paper, and putting the whole thing on the edge of the hot-plate where it will keep warm without overheating.

(continued on the next page)

Finishing the dish

4 Bring the nage (1) to the boil and add the crayfish tails (2), the beurre blanc (3) and the parsley and chervil sprigs and tarragon leaves. Bring back to the boil for an instant, taste and add more salt and pepper if necessary.

5 Divide the soup between two bowls or plates and place a crayfish head standing upright in the middle of each.

✳ Crayfish must be alive when you start. Once dead, they spoil very quickly and become inedible. You will generally find, in France, that the cultivated crayfish sold commercially have already been treated to relieve them of their black intestinal tract. However if you are using wild river crayfish you must remove it yourself. To do this, hold the crayfish by its head in one hand. Take the central fin of the tail between thumb and forefinger of the other hand, and pull it away sharply, giving it a little quarter turn as you do so. This should be done just before cooking, otherwise the crayfish will spoil rapidly.
Cultivated crayfish can be dealt with immediately after cooking if they still contain their intestinal tracts.

✳ This recipe is very practical since most of the cooking (or preparation) can be done the previous day, and the crayfish tails stored in the refrigerator in a little of the court-bouillon. The beurre blanc can be kept warm for up to an hour in the manner indicated above.

Gratin of Oysters with Champagne
Gratin de belons au champagne

For two people	Fairly simple Extremely expensive *Preparation time:* 45 minutes

Ingredients	12 oysters 100 g (3½ oz) raw spinach 3 tablespoons extra dry (Brut) champagne taken from the bottle to be drunk with the dish (cork it up well and put in refrigerator) 1 egg yolk 6 tablespoons chilled single cream 15 g (½ oz) butter a handful of seaweed 200 g (7 oz) coarse salt salt, pepper

Recommended wine	extra dry (Brut) champagne

1 Open the oysters and remove them carefully from their shells with a teaspoon, first cutting through the muscle that attaches them with a small sharp knife. These operations should be carried out over a strainer held over a small saucepan to catch the juices. Reserve the hollow halves of the shells. Add the 3 tablespoons champagne to the small pan, adding a little pepper. Bring to the boil, then reduce over a medium heat until no more than 2 tablespoons of liquid remain. Meanwhile plunge the oysters into very cold water for 15–20 seconds to firm them up, using a slotted spoon.

2 Pick over and trim the spinach and wash it thoroughly. Cook in a minimum of boiling salted water, uncovered, for 3–4 minutes. Refresh in cold water, drain and squeeze out the moisture. Chop coarsely with a knife.

(continued on the next page)

3 Spread 200 g (7 oz) coarse salt on a gratin dish which will fit under your grill, and set the concave shells firmly in it. Dry in a low oven for 5 minutes and keep hot.

4 Whisk the cream until it is slightly thick and add the egg yolk. Then whisk this mixture vigorously into the champagne reduction in the small saucepan (1). Heat through, whisking all the time, and *without boiling* – which would coagulate the egg and ruin the sauce. When the sauce has thickened a little, remove from the heat and taste for the seasoning.

5 Heat the grill until it is really hot. Meanwhile, reheat the spinach (2) with a nut of butter. Then put a little spinach in each hot shell (3), place an oyster on each and cover lightly with the sauce (4). Place the gratin dish under the grill until the sauce has formed a golden skin.

6 Make nests of seaweed on two large plates and plant six shells on each. Serve very hot.

✳ Be very careful not to oversalt this dish. The oyster juices are already salty. And take very great care not to boil the sauce in step (4), as it is easy to curdle it.

Editor's note
In France the seaweed used to line the plates of oysters is found in the barrels of oysters when they are delivered to restaurant or fishmonger. The variety used is young and tender Bladder Wrack (*Fiscus vesiculosus*), the fine type with small bubbles or bladders commonly found on the seashore.
If you live near the sea, gather it yourself at low tide and wash it well before use. If not you may be able to order it from your fishmonger. Failing this use oyster plates or small cocottes filled with gros sel and then heated through to serve your oysters.

Cockles with Still Champagne

Coques ou bucardes au vin nature de Champagne

For two people	Simple Inexpensive *Preparation time:* 15 minutes *Finishing time:* 15 minutes

Ingredients	2 litres (3½ pints) cockles in their shells (about 750 g (1¾ lb) in weight) 250 ml (scant half-pint) still Champagne 6 tablespoons whipping cream 20 g (¾ oz) butter 1 egg yolk 1 tablespoon finely-chopped shallots 1 heaped tablespoon chopped chervil 1 heaped tablespoon chopped parsley salt, pepper

Recommended wine	still Champagne

✳ Mussels and clams are both exceedingly good cooked in this way but as with all shellfish you must take great care not to over-cook them.

✳ This dish is best eaten with a spoon, and if not you should have a generous supply of bread to mop up the sauce. It is so good that you won't want to leave a single drop on your plate. Don't forget to put a large bowl on the table for the empty shells.

1 Wash the cockles, removing any small crabs and other undesirable tenants from the shells. Soak them in at least four fresh lots of cold water and drain in a colander.

2 Bring the champagne and the chopped shallot to the boil in a large saucepan. Throw in the cockles and cover the pan. Shake from time to time to make sure that none of the cockles are left too long in the liquid at the bottom of the pan. After about 10 minutes, when all the shells are open, tip the pan, keeping the lid on but just slightly open, and pour the cooking liquid into a smaller saucepan, taking care not to pour out all the liquid, as there are always traces of sand at the bottom of the pan. Keep the cockles warm in the pan.

3 Reduce the cooking liquid by boiling over a brisk heat until there are barely 3 tablespoons left. Then add 5 tablespoons of the cream and return to the boil. Meanwhile whisk the remaining cream and the egg yolk together thoroughly in a bowl. When the sauce has boiled, remove the pan from the heat and whisk in the egg/cream mixture. Allow to thicken over a very slow heat, without allowing the sauce to boil again, adding the butter little by little, in small pieces, whisking all the time. Add the chervil and parsley, taste and add a pinch of salt or pepper if necessary.

4 Remove the cockles with a slotted spoon (to avoid scooping up any of the sand), and arrange them in two deep plates. Coat with the sauce and serve.

Fricassee of Lobster with Sauternes Sauce

Fricassée de homard à la crème de Sauternes

For two people Fairly difficult
Extremely expensive
Preparation time: 1½ hours

Ingredients 2 small live lobsters weighing 500 g (1 lb 2 oz) each
8 tablespoons coarse salt
20 g (¾ oz) butter
150 ml (¼ pint) whipping cream
1 tablespoon carrot finely diced
1 tablespoon shallot finely diced
1 tablespoon celery finely diced
1 teaspoon tomato purée
1 tablespoon cognac
5 tablespoons Sauternes
a sprig of tarragon, about 8–10 leaves
a bunch of chervil, with the stalks removed
salt, pepper

Recommended wines I can only recommend a Sauternes with this dish, but there is of course the problem of which wine to serve next. You could perhaps pick a Chassagne-Montrachet or a fruity Pouilly fumé. You could also try one of the marvellous white Châteauneuf-du-Papes.

1 Despatch the lobsters in the way recommended on page 113. Bring 5 litres (9 pints) of water with 8 tablespoons of coarse salt to the boil and plunge in the lobsters. Cook at a rolling boil for 15 minutes, then remove from the heat. Leave the lobsters in the pan for a further 5 minutes. Then remove them and let them cool for 5–10 minutes.

2 The next stage is somewhat complicated so read the instructions carefully before you start and then read them again as you under-take each step.

    (a) Remove the claws. Bend the smaller, movable pincer back-wards till it comes away, bringing its cartilage with it. Crack the shell of the claw at the thickest part with the flat of a heavy knife without crushing it, in such a way that you can pull out the claw meat in one piece. Do the same with the small pincer. Put the flesh on one side and keep the pieces of shell.

    (b) Separate the 'rings' of the tail shell by rotating them in the opposite direction from their neighbours and taking care not to break them. Extract the flesh by cutting through the underside of the tail with a pair of stout kitchen scissors.

    (c) Remove all the legs, including the parts joining them to the underside of the head. Put 8 legs and one head on one side on a board.

You should now have: a plate containing the flesh of the claws and tails, a plate containing 8 legs and one whole head shell and a board containing the tail shells, the remaining legs, the parts join-ing all the legs to the head, the fragments of claw shell and the remaining head.

3 Crush the contents of the third plate, shells, legs and head, roughly with a cleaver or the back of a very large heavy knife.

4 Melt the butter in a saucepan and add the chopped carrot, shallot and celery. Allow to become golden over a moderate heat, then add the tomato purée. Mix carefully, and add the crushed carcases (3). Stir again and heat through for 3–4 minutes. Pour on the cognac and set it alight. When the flames have died down, add the Sau-ternes and reduce by half. Add the cream and the sprig of tarragon and reduce again over a moderate heat for 15 minutes. Salt lightly.

5 Strain the sauce through a fine wire sieve into another saucepan, pressing the lobster shells carefully with the back of a ladle to extract all the juices and cream. Taste and add a pinch of salt and pepper if necessary.

6 Just before serving, put the lobster flesh into the sauce and cook for a minute or two. Divide between two deep plates and decorate with the sprigs of chervil. Finish by garnishing each plate with 4 legs and half the reserved head (cut in half with scissors).

✳ Why mix lobsters, Sauternes and cream? Because, quite simply, all three have the same delicacy of flavour. The flesh of the lobster is so light on the palate that it is a great pity to overwhelm it with a powerful sauce. It is essential, in culinary matters, to respect the character of the ingredients that are being cooked.

Editor's note
Dealing with a live lobster at home is a problem – if possible ask your fishmonger to kill it for you and then hurry home and cook it. On a hot day take a cold insulated bag to carry it in. Remember that raw shellfish should be kept for a minimum of time as it deteriorates very rapidly. If you *are* stuck with doing the job yourself, however, the following method is probably the kindest. Take a cleaver or heavy knife and bang it down sharply where the shell of the head meets the body. This will kill the creature instantly.

Civet of Lobster in Burgundy
Homard en civet de vieux Bourgogne

For two people
Fairly simple
Extremely expensive
Preparation time: 45 minutes

Ingredients
1 live hen lobster weighing 1 kg (2¼ lb) for a main course **or** 350–400 g (12–14 oz) for a first course
2 tablespoons oil
70 g (2¾ oz) butter
2 shallots, chopped
½ carrot, cut into small dice
4 tablespoons cognac
¾ bottle red Burgundy, preferably Pommard, at least four years old
bouquet garni made up of 2 parsley sprigs, a small piece of celery, ½ bayleaf and a sprig of thyme
8 small button onions, peeled
pinch of icing sugar
10 small white button mushrooms
1 tablespoon flour
salt, pepper
chopped parsley for garnish

Recommended wine
the same wine as is used in preparing the dish

✳ This delicate but rustic-looking dish is perfectly accompanied by noodles (tagliatelle) cooked at the last moment and tossed in butter.

1 Despatch the lobster in the way recommended on page 113. Chop the tail part into six pieces and crush the claws lightly. Reserve the coral and creamy parts of the head, being careful to remove the sac, which should be clearly visible.

2 Season the pieces of lobster with salt and pepper and sauté rapidly in 2 tablespoons very hot oil. When the shells have turned a fiery red remove the pieces of lobster with a slotted spoon and keep on one side.

3 Put the pan back on the heat and add 25 g (1 oz) butter, the chopped shallots and diced carrot. Stir around gently, then put in the lobster pieces. Pour in the cognac and set it alight. When the flames have died down add the Burgundy and the bouquet garni. Season with salt and pepper and cover, simmer very gently over a low heat for 15 minutes.

4 Cook the little onions in a small saucepan with a little water, a nut of butter, salt and a pinch of icing sugar. They should brown without burning, the time will vary according to the size and age of the onions, so test them with a skewer or the point of a knife.

5 Sauté the mushrooms in a frying-pan with a nut of butter until golden and then drain them.

6 Put 50 g (1¾ oz) butter, the flour, and the coral and creamy head-parts of the lobster together in a bowl and work them to a smooth paste with a fork. This mixture will serve as the liaison for the sauce.

7 When the lobster is cooked (3), shell the pieces completely. Meanwhile reduce the cooking liquid by half. Arrange the lobster meat in two deep plates and strew with the little onions (4) and the mushrooms (5). Keep hot.

8 When the cooking liquid has reduced to half, lower the heat and, whisking all the time, incorporate enough of the liaison (6) to thicken the sauce to the right consistency. Taste and add a little salt if necessary, and three or four turns of the pepper-mill. Strain over the lobster, decorate with a pinch of chopped parsley and serve very hot.

Crawfish with Paprika

Langouste au poivre rose

For two people Fairly simple
Extremely expensive
Preparation time: 45 minutes for 2 crawfish, 55
 minutes for 1

Ingredients 2 live crawfish or spiny lobsters of 500 g (1 lb
 2 oz) each **or** one of 1 kg (2 lb 4 oz)
20 g ($\frac{3}{4}$ oz) butter
150 ml ($\frac{1}{4}$ pint) whipping cream
1 teaspoon sweet Hungarian paprika
1 tablespoon chopped shallot
1 small sprig tarragon
1 teaspoon tomato purée
3 tablespoons cognac
4 tablespoons dry white wine
1 tablespoon chopped chervil
salt, pepper

Recommended a dry white wine, slightly fruity, perhaps a
wines Pouilly fumé, a Sancerre, a Montrachet, a
 Puligny or a White Mâcon

1 Despatch the crawfish in the way recommended on page 113. Chop it in two lengthways with a cleaver. Remove the sac from the head.

2 Melt the butter with the chopped shallot in a large sauté pan, and when the shallot has softened, add the paprika, mixing it in well to break up any little lumps. Stir in the tomato purée. Place the pieces of crawfish, flesh downwards, in the sauce and let them seal over a moderate heat before flaming with the cognac to sear the shells. Pour in the wine and add the sprig of tarragon, then turn the crawfish halves over, so that they are shell side downwards, cover the pan and cook over a slow heat for 20 minutes if you have 2 crawfish and 30 minutes if you have only one. Take care that the liquid in the pan does not reduce too far: if it does, add 1 or 2 tablespoons of water.

3 When they are cooked, remove the crawfish. Remove the tail shells and put the halves in two deep plates. Keep hot.

4 Return the pan to the heat and reduce the liquid to 1 or 2 tablespoons. Add 150 ml ($\frac{1}{4}$ pint) cream and boil for 5 minutes to thicken the sauce. Taste for seasoning and add salt and pepper if necessary. Strain the sauce through a fine wire sieve and add the chervil. Pour over the crawfish and serve with plain boiled rice.

✱ Small crawfish, or spiny lobsters as they are also known, are tenderer than larger ones, so you will be well advised to opt for two specimens of 500 g (1 lb 2 oz) for this recipe. Choose the red crawfish – called 'royales' in France – or else the pink crawfish from the Atlantic, if you have a choice. But whatever you do, make sure they are alive and kicking because once they are dead their juices spoil very quickly and the flesh loses its quality and texture.

✱ If you buy your live crawfish in advance, tuck the tails under the bodies, roll them up tightly in a newspaper and store in the vegetable compartment of the refrigerator. Be careful, as too low a temperature will kill them.

Grilled Crawfish with Basil Butter

Langouste grillée au beurre de basilic

For two people   Simple
Extremely expensive
Preparation time: 5 minutes
Cooking time: 30 minutes for 1 crawfish, 20 minutes for 2

Ingredients   2 live crawfish or spiny lobsters of 500 g (1 lb 2 oz) **or** one of 1 kg (2 lb 4 oz)
100 g (3½ oz) butter
20 leaves of basil, roughly chopped
2 tablespoons olive oil
salt, pepper

Recommended wines   fresh dry white wines, such as Graves, Sancerre, and Côtes de Provence

1 Preheat the grill. Despatch the crawfish in the way recommended on page 113, and split them in two lengthways. Put the crawfish halves on a roasting dish small enough to fit under the grill. Season the flesh with salt and pepper and sprinkle with olive oil. Then, grill them for 5 minutes on the flesh side and 5 minutes on the shell side. (If you are using a barbecue, cook them shell side downwards for 5 minutes first, then flesh side downwards for a further 5 minutes.) Meanwhile put the butter with the basil in a small saucepan and let it melt over a low heat.

2 Turn the crawfish halves flesh side up and sprinkle liberally with the butter and basil. Without turning them, continue to cook the crawfish for 10 minutes more for 2 small ones or 20 minutes for one large one, basting frequently with the basil butter.

3 Serve with no further embellishment. The butter will have 'nourished' the flesh and perfumed it with the subtle fragrance of basil.

Scallops with Leeks

Noix de Saint-Jacques aux poireaux

For two people Fairly simple
Moderately expensive
Preparation time: 1 hour

Ingredients 6 scallops in their shells (about 2 kg (4½ lb))
4 thin young leeks – about 200 g (7 oz)
1 teaspoon chopped shallot
3 generous tablespoons double cream
25 g (1 oz) butter
1 bunch chervil, stalks removed
2 tablespoons dry white vermouth
3 tablespoons of the white wine you have chosen for the meal
salt, pepper

Recommended wines a fruity Pouilly fumé, Chassagne or Puligny

1 Open the scallops by sliding a small sharp knife between the top and bottom shells and carefully cutting through the muscle which holds the flat shell in place. Remove each scallop from the concave shell with a teaspoon and remove the spongy beard so that you have only the white 'noix' and the orange coral (if any) from which you should detach the black sac. Wash the scallops in several waters to remove every trace of sand, and dry carefully on a towel or kitchen paper. Throw out the trimmings and shells.

2 Trim and clean the leeks, cutting off the roots, taking off the outside layer and cutting off the green part. Split them in half lengthways. Wash very carefully under the tap, using tepid water to dissolve any mud more easily, and shake vigorously to drain them. Then cut into little narrow strips 3–4 cm (1¼–1½ inches) long, and put with 15 g (½ oz) of the butter and 4 tablespoons water in a small saucepan. Salt lightly, cover and cook for 20 minutes over a slow heat, stirring from time to time with a wooden spoon. Set on one side and keep hot.

3 Cut each scallop in two horizontally, leaving the corals whole. Melt the remaining butter with the chopped shallot in a small saucepan and add the scallops and their corals. Cover with the vermouth and white wine. Do not add salt. Bring to the boil and simmer for 2 minutes, then remove the scallops with a slotted spoon and keep hot with the leeks.

4 Return the saucepan in which the scallops have cooked to the heat, and allow to reduce briskly. Add the cooking juices from the leeks, and reduce until there is no more than 3–4 tablespoons of liquid left. Then add the cream and bring briefly to the boil. Taste for seasoning and add salt and pepper if necessary, then strain the sauce over the scallops and leeks. Sprinkle sprigs of chervil over the top, divide between hot bowls or deep plates and serve immediately.

Braised Chicken Turbot with Sorrel
Turbotin braisé à l'oseille

For two people	Simple
	Moderately expensive
	Preparation time: preparing the fish, several hours; assembling the dish, 20 minutes
	Cooking and finishing time: 35 minutes

Ingredients	1 chicken turbot of 1 kg (2¼ lb)
	6 tablespoons dry white wine
	2 shallots
	5 tablespoons double cream
	2 bunches sorrel – 80 g (3 oz) in all
	30 g (1¼ oz) butter at room temperature
	salt, pepper

Recommended wine	a young dry white wine, which can also be used in the recipe

Preparation

1 Clean the turbot and remove the gills. Cut away the fins from each side. Prepare the fish by soaking it in very cold, even iced, water for 5–6 hours. Dry it on a towel or kitchen paper.

2 Preheat the oven to 200°C/400°F/Mark 6. Peel and chop the shallots finely. Remove the tough central ribs of the sorrel by pulling the tender green parts away from each side. Wash and drain the sorrel, then roll each leaf up like a cigar and cut each roll into very fine slices, in order to obtain thin ribbons, or a 'chiffonade'.

(continued on the next page)

Cooking

3 Season the turbot on both sides with salt and pepper. Cover the bottom of a baking-dish with 10 g ($\frac{1}{3}$ oz) of butter and sprinkle it with the chopped shallot. Place the turbot on top with the dark skin uppermost. Pour the white wine over the fish and cook in the hot oven for 20–25 minutes. To tell when it is cooked, press your index finger down firmly on the backbone, just below the head. If you can feel the bone, the fish is cooked.

4 Put the cooked fish on one side to keep hot and pour the cooking juices and shallots into a saucepan with sloping sides. Reduce over a brisk heat until no more than 2–3 tablespoons of syrupy liquid remains. Pour in the cream, return to the heat and bring briefly to the boil. Throw in the 'chiffonade' of sorrel and stir it in carefully with a wooden spatula. Bring back to the boil, taste and season with salt and pepper. Away from the heat, add the remaining butter little by little, beating continuously with the wooden spatula. When all the butter has been incorporated, set the sauce on one side to keep warm.

5 Remove the black skin from the turbot – it should peel off very easily. Then remove all the little bones from the flat fin running round the edge of the fish. This is simply done by running a sharp knife round the fish between the flesh and the fin and pushing the bones outwards. You will then have a turbot divested of its dark skin and fringe of bones, but retaining its head. Place it on a hot, lightly buttered serving-dish and put to keep hot in the oven, turned off and with the door open.

6 To serve the turbot, simply cover it lightly with the sorrel sauce (**4**), leaving only the head without sauce, and serve the rest of the sauce separately.

John Dory with Spring Vegetables

Blanc de Saint-Pierre à la crème de petits légumes

For two people	Fairly simple Moderately expensive *Preparation time:* 30 minutes *Cooking time:* 15 minutes

Ingredients

1 John Dory weighing 800 g–1 kg (1¾ lb–2¼ lb) **or** the same weight of fillets of sole, monk-fish, turbot, bass, etc.
1 medium carrot
1 white part of a leek
the innermost white heart of a head of celery
1 medium potato
20 very tiny French beans
1 bunch chives
6 tablespoons double cream
30 g (1 oz) butter
salt, pepper

Recommended wines   mellow white wines such as Mâcon, Burgundy, and Provençal blanc de blancs.

Preparation

1 If you have a friendly fishmonger, ask him to fillet the John Dory for you. If not, clean the fish, wash it and place it flat on a chopping board. With the point of a small sharp knife, pierce the skin at the inner edge of the encircling bony fringe and trace the outline of the fish all the way round, as if you were re-drawing it, but 1 cm (bare ½ inch) in from the edge. Then run the point of the knife from the head to the tail along the backbone. Slide the knife under the flesh flat against the bones on both sides and lift off the fillets. Turn the fish over and do the same on the other side. You will have obtained 4 handsome fillets – and will probably have decided to change your fishmonger by now.

To skin the fillets, place them skin-side down on the chopping board. Starting at the tail end, and keeping the skin flat against the board, run your very sharp knife carefully to and fro between the skin and the flesh until the latter is completely free. Cut each fillet into strips the size of your index finger and set aside. Repeat with the other three fillets.

2 Peel the carrot and trim the leek and celery. Wash all three and cut them into coarse julienne strips about the size of the prong of a carving fork. Peel and wash the potato and cut in large dice. Put it in a small saucepan with lightly salted water to cover. Top and tail the French beans and wash them. Cook in a large pan of boiling salted water for 4–5 minutes. Remove from the heat when they are still slightly crisp and refresh in cold water. Drain and keep on one side.

3 Chop the chives finely and keep them on one side.

Cooking
4 Put the potato (2) on to cook until tender.

5 Put the julienne vegetables (2) into a small saucepan with a pinch of salt, 3 tablespoons water and a teaspoon of butter. Cover and allow to cook on a brisk heat until the carrots are tender and the water has almost evaporated. These vegetables too should have a slight bite to them. The whole operation should take less than 10 minutes. Keep the cooked vegetables hot.

6 Pour the cream into a saucepan, salt lightly and add the strips of John Dory (1). Bring to the boil and simmer for 2 minutes – not a second more!

7 Place a strainer over the container of the liquidiser and drain the cream into it. Put the drained fillets in the pan with the julienne vegetables and the beans, which should be completely dry. Add half the cooked potato dice (4) to the cooking juices in the liquidiser and purée until you have a smooth light sauce. If it seems too thin, add a little more potato. Add the remaining butter and blend again briefly. Season with salt and pepper if necessary.

8 Pour the light sauce over the fish and vegetables in the saucepan and bring rapidly to the boil. Stir in the chopped chives and serve at once in deep plates.

✳ In this recipe you will discover the delicacy and velvety texture of a completely natural sauce.

Bourride from Agde

Petite bourride agathoise

For two people	Fairly simple Extremely expensive *Preparation time:* 45 minutes

Ingredients	1 live crawfish of 500 g (1 lb 2 oz) 250 g (8¾ oz) fillet of monkfish 4 fillets from a small sole of 400 g (14½ oz) 2 tablespoons chopped onion ½ teaspoon tomato purée 1 clove of garlic 1 sprig thyme 1 small bayleaf 1 small branch of dried fennel 6 tablespoons olive oil 1 egg yolk 20 g (¾ oz) butter 2 tablespoons chopped parsley 8 slices of French bread ½ cm (¼ inch) thick 2 tablespoons cognac or armagnac 5 tablespoons dry white vermouth 6 tablespoons dry white wine salt, pepper

Recommended wines	white wines from the Côtes de Provence or white Graves

1 Skin the monkfish and cut it in half. Make incisions in the skin side of each sole fillet and fold them in two, with the incisions inside.

2 Despatch the crawfish in the way recommended on page 113. (If anyone offers to sell you a dead crustacean, don't touch it. Whatever you pay will be too much as you won't be able to do anything with it.) Take a stout pair of kitchen scissors and cut off the legs of the crawfish and put them on one side. It is important not to start dismembering the crawfish until the last moment, less than 10 minutes before you want to cook it.

3 Put 2 tablespoons olive oil and 2 tablespoons chopped onion into a 25 cm (10 inch) shallow saucepan and let them turn pale golden, stirring with a wooden spatula. Add the tomato purée and mix well. Add the crushed clove of garlic – flattened with the blade of a knife – then the thyme, bayleaf and fennel and the legs of the crawfish. Arrange the two crawfish halves, shell sides down, and the monkfish fillets on this bed, and spread out the sole fillets on top. Flame with the cognac or armagnac, and when the flames have died down add the vermouth and white wine. Do not add salt. Cover the pan and cook for 5 minutes over a medium heat, then add 3 tablespoons or more of hot water. Continue to cook for 10 minutes more then remove the saucepan from the heat and set aside in a warm place, covered.

4 While the fish and crawfish are cooking, put the egg yolk into a large bowl with 2 tablespoons of tepid water. Whisk well, then gradually add 4 tablespoons of olive oil in a thin stream, whisking constantly as though you are making a mayonnaise.

5 Melt the butter in a frying-pan and fry the slices of bread until they are a pretty pale golden colour. Set aside on a plate to keep hot.

6 Arrange the crawfish halves and legs and the fillets of monkfish and sole carefully on two hot soup plates. Cover with two more plates and keep hot. Strain the cooking liquid through a fine wire sieve into the bowl containing the egg/oil emulsion (4), whisking gently throughout and pressing down the debris to extract the

juices. Wash out the saucepan and pour the contents of the bowl into it. Still whisking, replace it over a moderate heat. Take the pan off the heat before it boils or the egg will coagulate, whereas the object is to thicken the liquid lightly. Stir in the chopped parsley and season with salt and pepper. Divide the liquid between the two plates and serve as soon as possible, with the croûtons (5) handed separately.

✳ Sole and monkfish can be replaced by other white fish, so long as their flesh is firm. For instance, John Dory, red mullet, gurnard, sea-bass, scorpion-fish (chapon) and various types of bream would all be suitable.

✳ This recipe was given to me by Raymond Vidal at the time he was promoting the good life at the Club de Cavalière Restaurant, near Lavandou, when I was chef. He had inherited the recipe, he told me, from his mother, who had cooked it so marvellously that no chef in the world could recreate the dish for him exactly as he remembered it. The problem was the recipe had never been written down, and survived only in his memory of it. And that changed slightly from week to week. We often argued passionately about some ingredient or other which I thought utterly incongruous and he declared to be absolutely indispensable 'because my mother always put it in'. From time to time he would taste my efforts, and, hands behind his back, would grunt 'not enough salt'. To please him, I would pretend to add salt. Then, one day, a mischievous scullion, seeing a damp spoon dangling in his hands, put a big pinch of salt in it. Raymond Vidal, thinking that I had only pretended to add salt to the pot, tasted another spoonful, practically choked and bravely announced 'much better'. After that, he left me alone in the kitchen to make his mother's bourride in my own way.

John Dory as Cooked by the Suquet Fishermen

Saint-Pierre des pêcheurs du Suquet

For two people	Simple Moderately expensive *Preparation time:* 1½ hours

Ingredients	1 John Dory weighing 1 kg (2¼ lb), filleted (see page 123) but not skinned 1 large onion weighing 180 g (6½ oz) 2 large waxy potatoes weighing 400 g (14 oz) 2 cloves of garlic 1 sprig thyme 1 bayleaf 1 pinch saffron 2 large ripe tomatoes, weighing 80 g (3 oz) apiece 40 g (1½ oz) butter 1 stock cube salt, pepper

Recommended wines	fresh young wines, Provençal red, white or rosé

1 Preheat the oven to 200°C/400°F/Mark 6. Peel the onion and slice it into fine rounds. Melt 15 g ($\frac{1}{2}$ oz) of butter in a frying-pan and soften the onions in it over a slow heat until they begin to turn golden.

2 Bring 6 tablespoons of water to the boil in a small saucepan and dissolve the stock cube, together with the pinch of saffron. Set aside.

3 Peel the potatoes and wipe them (do not wash them). Slice them into paper-thin slices (3–4 mm thick), spread them out on a cloth or kitchen paper, and season with salt and pepper. Crush the cloves of garlic without peeling them. Slice the tomatoes without peeling them.

4 Butter the inside of a gratin dish 20–25 cm (8–10 inches) long and arrange a single layer of potato slices in it, followed by the onion cooked in butter (1). Lay the John Dory fillets, seasoned with salt and pepper on both sides, on top, and the tomato slices on top of that. Put a crushed clove of garlic at each end of the dish, and lay the thyme and bayleaf on the tomatoes. Cover the whole dish with the remaining potato slices. Cut the remaining butter into small pieces and dot them over the top, pour over the saffron-flavoured stock (2), and bake uncovered in the oven for 1 hour. Serve in the gratin dish. The liquid will have evaporated and the dish will be covered with a beautiful golden crust.

✳ I first had this dish with the fishermen of the Quai Saint-Pierre in Cannes. They had arranged two handsome John Dorys, with their monstrous heads, in two large tians. (A tian is a glazed terra-cotta dish which is used for any dish that is to be roasted, gratinéd or simmered in the oven.) With its potatoes gilded with saffron, ruddy tomatoes, pale onions, bluish thyme, green bayleaf and steel-grey fish, all in their brown dishes, it made a magnificent sight in the May sunlight. The two tians were carried off to the local baker's oven and reappeared an hour and a half later crusted with gold, and giving out the most extraordinary, powerful yet subtle aroma, such as you cannot possibly imagine. There were ten of us and we ate standing up – as it deserved.

Baked Sea-Bream with Bayleaves and a Fondue of Oranges and Lemons

Daurade royale rôtie au laurier avec sa fondue d'orange et de citron à l'huile d'olive

For two people	Simple
	Moderately expensive
	Preparation time: 50 minutes

Ingredients	1 royal or gilt-head sea-bream of 800 g–1 kg (1¾–2¼ lb)
	3 seedless oranges
	2 lemons
	6 generous tablespoons olive oil
	5 bayleaves, preferably fresh
	salt, pepper

Recommended wine	Still Champagne

✳ In this recipe the sharpness of the lemon is tempered by the sweetness of the orange and the olive oil. It is a summer dish, a recipe for a sunny day. The same fruit sauce could also be served with a grilled fish.

✳ The gilt-head or royal bream, one of the most noble fishes of the Mediterranean, is recognised by its steel-grey colour and especially by its snub-nosed convex head, topped with a small golden bump.

✳ Lesser fishes can also be prepared in the same manner, for instance, sea-bass and humbler members of the bream family.

1 Preheat the oven to 250°C/500°F/Mark 10. If possible, have the bream gutted and scaled by your fishmonger. Cut 3 bayleaves into eight little triangles (twenty-four in all). Salt and pepper the fish lavishly, inside and out. Then, *without* piercing the flesh beneath, make twelve horizontal incisions in the skin on each side with a small sharp knife, and slide a triangle of bayleaf into each. Then massage the fish with your fingertips, from head to tail, to help the flavours to permeate the flesh. Finally place 2 bayleaves inside the fish. Sprinkle with olive oil – 1 tablespoon for each side – and rub the oil in thoroughly with your hands or with a pastry-brush. Half fill a roasting-tin with hot water and place the bream on a wire rack in the tin.

2 Place the roasting tin in the oven and bake the fish for 15 minutes on one side and 10 on the other. This time may vary slightly according to the size of the fish. You can test whether the fish is cooked by sliding the point of a knife into the spine, just behind the head. If the flesh comes away from the bone cleanly and easily, the fish is done.

3 While the bream is cooking, peel the oranges and lemons with a very sharp knife, taking care to remove every trace of white pith. Hold the fruit over a small saucepan to catch the juices, and separate the quarters, removing the inner skins.

4 Add the peeled segments to the juices in the saucepan and add 3 generous tablespoons of olive oil. Season with salt and pepper and heat through before serving. Be careful not to let the fruit get too hot, or it will disintegrate.

5 Serve the fish on a long dish, and the fruit in a sauceboat.

Sea-Bass Fillets with Lettuce Leaves

Suprême de loup au vert de laitue

For four people	Fairly simple Rather expensive *Preparation time:* 45 minutes
Ingredients	1 sea-bass weighing 1.5 kg (3¼ lb) 2 nice green lettuces, not too tightly curled 1 tablespoon chopped shallot 3 generous tablespoons dry white wine 3 tablespoons dry white vermouth 3 tablespoons whipping cream 1 egg yolk 70 g (2½ oz) butter a trickle of oil 2 tablespoons flour salt, pepper
Recommended wines	White wines such as Graves, Hermitage blanc, Meursault

✳ This recipe, simple and made from easily obtained ingredients, is a fine example of the search for a sensitive balance of flavours and subtlety of detail. The lettuce leaves keep the fish succulent and at the same time impart a slightly bitter note, which is underlined by the vermouth. The flavour of the white wine marries with that of the shallots. Searing the fish before wrapping it in lettuce leaves preserves all its juices.

✳ The bass is one of the most delicate and fine-textured of fish. In this recipe it can, however, be replaced by fillets of bream, hake, pollack, pike-perch or even pike. The most important thing is the freshness of the fish – and of course, the quality of the sauce.

1 If a friendly fishmonger has not already done it for you, gut and scale the fish and remove the fillets, then skin them carefully (see instructions page 123). Cut each fillet into two. Season with salt and pepper and sprinkle with flour. Heat 15 g ($\frac{1}{2}$ oz) of butter and a trickle of oil in a frying-pan and brown the fillets briefly, 1 minute on each side over a brisk heat. Put on one side. Preheat the oven to 170°C/325°F/Mark 3.

2 Put 2 litres ($3\frac{1}{2}$ pints) water on to boil, and meanwhile detach the outer leaves of the lettuces and wash them, together with the hearts. When the water boils, plunge in the outer lettuce leaves and remove them almost immediately with a slotted spoon. Refresh in cold water and drain. Next plunge the lettuce hearts into the same boiling water for 5 minutes, then refresh and drain. Cut each heart in half vertically, and flatten them slightly. Carefully dry the outer leaves with kitchen paper and wrap them round the bass fillets (1).

3 Butter a gratin dish large enough to contain the fillets, and strew it with the chopped shallots. Cover them with a bed of the flattened lettuce hearts. Arrange the four lettuce-wrapped fillets of bass on this bed, pour the white wine and vermouth over them and cook for 12 minutes in the medium oven.

4 When they are cooked, drain the bass fillets, still in their green lettuce wrappings, and the lettuce hearts, and arrange them on a serving dish, putting the lettuce hearts underneath the fish. Keep hot.

5 Pour the cooking juices into a saucepan, put it over a fierce heat and reduce until there is no more than 2 tablespoons left. Beat the cream and the egg yolk together in a bowl and whisk this mixture into the reduction away from the heat. Return to the heat, whisking all the time, and remove just before the sauce comes to the boil. Incorporate the remaining butter little by little in small pieces whisking continuously. Taste for seasoning. Pour the sauce over the bass fillets and serve.

Small Red Mullet, Pierrot's Way

Les petits rougets de mon ami Pierrot

For two people	Simple
	Moderately expensive
	Preparation time: marination, 8 hours
	Cooking and finishing the dish: 30 minutes

Ingredients	500 g (1 lb 2 oz) small red mullet
	5 anchovy fillets preserved in oil
	2 oranges and 1 lemon
	10 crushed peppercorns
	150 ml (¼ pint) best virgin olive oil
	2 tablespoons flour
	1 small bulb of fennel
	8 thin slices of French bread
	2 cloves garlic
	salt, pepper

Recommended wines	Côtes de Provence blanc or other dry white wine

✻ This dish can be eaten cold, but on no account put it in the refrigerator. In that case serve the fennel purée cold as well, in a separate bowl. The first time I had this dish it was made by my fisherman friend Pierrot. We drank a white wine from Saint-Tropez, cool from the well, and toasted big slices of pain de campagne at a fire on which a bouillabaisse was bubbling away. It was very simple, but no feast on earth could make me forget that meal.

✻ Red mullet should not be more than the length of a small person's hand, and if you are lucky enough to live by the Mediterranean, choose fish that have been caught that morning. The red mullet is a beautiful rosy-red shot with gold. Good quality Atlantic red mullet are also, however, excellent and can be used perfectly well for this recipe.

Marinating the fish

1 Scale and gut the fish, taking care to leave in the liver if you are using real red mullet. Prick each mullet here and there with a needle. Arrange them in a deep dish and cover with 6 tablespoons olive oil. Add the coarsely crushed peppercorns and one of the oranges cut into thin slices. Cover with a cloth and leave to marinate in a cool place (but not in the refrigerator) for not less than 8 hours. The mullet will become impregnated with the delicate flavour of the oil and the aroma of the orange.

Cooking and finishing the dish

2 Wash the fennel and cut it into four pieces. Put to cook in a small saucepan with 1 litre (1¾ pints) cold water, the juice of the lemon and a little salt. When it is tender liquidise the fennel with a tablespoon of olive oil or sieve it through a mouli-légumes and then mix in the oil. Season with salt and pepper and keep hot.

3 Rub the 8 slices of bread with garlic and fry in 2 tablespoons olive oil. Keep hot.

4 Half an hour before they are to be cooked, drain the mullet, taking care to keep the marinade, part of which will be used later. Wipe the fish, season them with salt and pepper and dust them lightly with flour.
Heat 3 tablespoons of the marinade in the frying-pan and when it is hot put in the mullet. Two minutes cooking on each side is quite enough if the fish are to remain moist. Arrange them on a dish, well separated, and throw away the oil in which they were cooked.

5 Heat another 3 tablespoons of the marinade, together with the anchovies, lightly crushed with a fork, and the juice of half an orange in the frying-pan. Season with pepper, stir carefully and pour the sauce over the mullet. Spread the fried croûtons (3) with the fennel purée (2) and serve with the mullet.

Escalopes of Fresh Salmon Marinated with Basil

Escalopes de saumon frais, mariné à l'huile de basilic

For two people Simple
Extremely expensive
Preparation time: 20 minutes

300–400 g (10½–14½ oz) very fresh tail-cut of salmon
200 g (7 oz) fresh white button mushrooms
1 tablespoon chopped parsley
10 handsome leaves of basil or 1 teaspoon chopped dill (or you can omit the herbs altogether and serve the salmon 'au nature')
5 tablespoons olive oil
juice of one-and-a-half lemons
fine salt, freshly-ground white pepper

Recommended wines dry white wines – Côtes du Rhône, Pouilly-Fuissé

1 Ask your fishmonger to fillet a tail cut of salmon weighing 300–400 g. If he won't, scale the tail yourself and remove the fillets, cutting through the skin down either side of the backbone and then repeating on the stomach side. Remove any little bones from the base of the fins. Slice the fillets into very fine escalopes with a very sharp knife without cutting into the skin which is carefully removed. The slices should be as thin as smoked salmon.

2 Lay the slices flat on 2 chilled plates without allowing them to overlap. Sprinkle with the juice of a lemon, and season with fine salt, and several turns of the pepper-mill. Cut the basil leaves into fine strips and divide them between the two plates or scatter the dill over the salmon slices. Pour $1\frac{1}{2}$ tablespoons olive oil over each plate. This step must not be carried out more than 30 minutes before the salmon is to be served.

3 Remove the stalks from 200 g (7 oz) button mushrooms, wash them well and cut them in fine slices. Put them in a bowl and season with salt, pepper, 2 tablespoons olive oil, the juice of half a lemon and 1 tablespoon chopped parsley. Just before serving, arrange a fan of the seasoned mushroom slices on each plate of salmon, or alternatively serve the mushrooms on a separate dish.

✳ This is a very delicate dish, and makes a simple and pleasant cold first course. Don't throw away the salmon skin. Cut it in thin strips, salt it and let it crisp, without fat, in a frying-pan. Season generously with pepper and serve with drinks, or separately with the marinated salmon.

Escalopes of Fresh Salmon Marinière

Escalopes de saumon frais en marinière

For two people Fairly simple
Moderately expensive
Preparation time: 20 minutes
Cooking and finishing: 15 minutes

Ingredients 2 fresh salmon escalopes of 100 g (3½ oz) each
(these are skinless and look like neat veal
escalopes)
2 handsome Dublin Bay prawns
2 scallops
8 mussels
150 ml (¼ pint) dry white wine – Burgundy or
Pouilly fumé
1 tablespoon dry vermouth
1 shallot, chopped
the white part of 2 leeks
110 g (3¾ oz) butter
1 bunch of chervil leaves (with stalks removed)
salt, freshly-ground pepper

Recommended wines Pouilly fumé, white Burgundy

✳ This is a marvellously fresh dish which will make your mouth
water even before it reaches the table.

1 Scrape and clean the mussels and wash them well. Put them in a saucepan with one tablespoon of water. Cover the pan and place it over a fierce heat to open the mussels. Shake the pan frequently. They should cook very quickly. When they are all open remove one shell from each mussel. Keep the mussels and their juice on one side.

2 Shell and wash the two scallops (with their coral) under running water and slice the white parts into three horizontally.

3 Shell the tails of the uncooked Dublin Bay prawns.

4 Put the white wine into a medium-sized saucepan and add the chopped shallot, the vermouth and the juice from the mussels (1). Add pepper and simmer over a moderate heat for ten minutes, then keep this 'fond' hot.

5 Cut the white part of two leeks into little strips 3 cm (1¼ inches) long and 4 mm (⅕ inch) wide and wash and drain them. Season this 'julienne' with salt and pepper, and let it soften in 15 g (½ oz) of butter and 2 tablespoons of water in a small covered pan for 15 minutes over a gentle heat. Keep hot.

6 Return the saucepan with the 'fond' (4) to the heat, and in it place the salmon escalopes, the scallops (2), the Dublin Bay prawn tails (3) and the half-shelled mussels, spacing everything out well. Cover, bring to simmering point and cook gently for exactly 1 minute. Meanwhile divide the cooked julienne of leeks (5) between two large heated deep plates. Then, remove the fish and shellfish quickly from the pan with a slotted spoon and arrange them on the bed of leeks. Cover each one with another plate and keep it hot.

7 Reduce the cooking liquid rapidly over a brisk heat until there are about 6 tablespoons left. While it is still boiling, add 100 g (3½ oz) butter in little pieces, whisking until the juices and butter have blended into a smooth sauce. Taste for seasoning and pour over the fish. Strew with little sprigs of chervil and serve immediately, accompanied only by toasted slices of pain de campagne.

Fricassee of Sole with Mussels and Saffron

Fricassée de sole aux moules à la crème de safran

For two people	Fairly simple Moderately expensive *Preparation time:* 1 hour 20 minutes

---

Ingredients

One 500 g (1 lb 2 oz) sole filleted by the fish-monger

500 g (1 lb 2 oz) mussels (preferably the very small ones called in France 'moules de Bouchot')

20 g (¾ oz) butter

6 tablespoons whipping cream

1 potato of 150 g (5½ oz)

1 leek of 70 g (2½ oz)

1 carrot of 70 g (2½ oz)

1 inner branch of celery

70 g (2½ oz) shelled petits pois **or** tiny French beans

1 tablespoon chopped shallot

2 tablespoons chopped parsley

5 tablespoons dry white wine from the bottle you are serving with the dish

1 pinch of whole saffron stamens

salt, freshly-ground pepper

Recommended wines

dry white wine such as Sauvignon, Vin de Palette, Meursault

---

1 Peel the potato and cut it in six pieces. Cook in plenty of boiling lightly salted water for 15–20 minutes, as if you were preparing mashed potatoes. When it is cooked, put the pieces to drain in the mouli-légumes. Throw out the cooking water, clean and dry the saucepan and place the mouli-légumes over it. Sieve the potato and, immediately stir in 20 g (¾ oz) butter. Work well with a wooden spatula in order to obtain a very smooth purée. Set on one side in a bowl.

2 While the potato is cooking, wash the leek and the celery and peel the carrot. Cut all three into large julienne strips and cook in 1 litre (1¾ pints) boiling salted water. When the vegetables are cooked, but still slightly firm, put them to drain in a colander.

3 If you are using French beans, top and tail them and cut into short lengths. Whether you are using beans or petits pois, plunge them into 1 litre (1¾ pints) boiling salted water and cook them un-covered (you must *never* cover green vegetables during cooking) for 5 minutes for petits pois and 10 minutes for French beans. Drain them in the colander with the other vegetables (2).

4 Scrape and clean the mussels and wash them in several waters. Place them in a large saucepan with the chopped shallot and dry white wine. Cover the pan and cook briskly, shaking the pan from time to time to move the mussels about. Cook for 5–10 minutes or until all the mussels are open. Remove them with a slotted spoon and allow to cool on a plate. Keep the cooking liquid. When the mussels have cooled, shell them and keep them on one side.

5 Cut the fillets of sole into strips the length of your little finger. Strain the mussel liquid (4) through a fine strainer into a saucepan, keeping back the last few tablespoons, which may be sandy. Reduce this liquid until there is no more than 3 tablespoons left. Add the cream and the fillets of sole and bring briefly to the boil. Take out the strips of sole with a slotted spoon and put them in the colander with the vegetables and the mussels.

6 Bring the liquid in which the sole has cooked back to the boil then add the potato purée (1), a spoonful at a time, whisking all the time. Whisk till the sauce is perfectly smooth (or alternatively purée it in the liquidiser to give an even more velvety texture).

7 When you want to eat the dish turn the contents of the colander (vegetables, mussels and sole) into the sauce. Taste and season with pepper – and salt if the mussels have not provided enough. Add a pinch of saffron and the chopped parsley. Bring up to boiling point and serve in deep, heated plates.

Goujonettes of Sole with Artichoke Hearts

Goujonettes de sole aux coeurs d'artichauts

For two people	Simple Moderately expensive *Preparation time:* 30 minutes

Ingredients	1 sole of 600 g (1 lb 5 oz) filleted by the fishmonger 4 handsome purple artichokes 1 lemon 1 large waxy potato weighing 100–120 g (3½–4¼ oz) 4 tablespoons flour 4 tablespoons milk 50 g (1¾ oz) butter 3 tablespoons olive oil 2 tablespoons chopped parsley salt, pepper

Recommended wines	white wine from the Var, Palette or any other dry white wine

1 Snap off the stems of the artichokes, which should break cleanly, taking all their fibre with them (unless extremely young) – a test of their freshness. Wash the artichokes by plunging them up and down head first in a bowl of cold water. This will wash out any tiny snails or other undesirables which may have crept down between the leaves. Drain. Bring 3 litres (5¼ pints) of water to the boil with a small handful of coarse salt and when it boils plunge in the artichokes. Do not cover, and cook over a fierce heat for about 20 minutes. Then pull out one of the centre leaves; if its edible base is cooked but still a little crisp, the artichokes are ready. (If you find it difficult to remove a leaf, allow to cook for a little longer and try again.) When they are cooked plunge the artichokes into cold water for 4–5 minutes and then drain them. Remove the leaves, discarding all but the best, which you can keep to nibble as you cook. Remove the chokes, cut the hearts into eight pieces, as if you were cutting a tart and set them aside on a plate.

2 Your fishmonger will have filleted and skinned your sole (if not, the method is much the same as that for filleting John Dory, page 123). Spread out the fillets and cut them across the grain diagonally, starting at the tail end, into ribbons about the width of your little finger. Put them into a deep dish, cover with milk and leave to rest.

3 Peel the potato and dry it in a cloth. Slice as if you were making thin chips, 7 mm (¼ inch) thick and 4–5 cm (2 inches) long. Rinse in water (but do not soak or they will be leathery) and dry them on a cloth.

4 Put 1½ tablespoons olive oil and 20 g (¾ oz) butter in each of two heavy frying-pans. Half-fill a soup plate with flour; take out the fillets of sole (2) and shake them dry, then plunge them in the flour and stir them around thoroughly so that each fillet is covered with flour. Then, taking one fillet at a time, and using the flat of your hand, roll them on a wooden board so that they look like nicely-rounded goujonettes.

5 Heat both frying-pans and wait for the moment when the oil/ butter mixture has ceased to hiss, which tells you that it has reached the right temperature. Put the potato chips in one pan and the sole

(*continued on the next page*)

goujonettes in the other, stirring both alternately with a wooden spatula. Let the goujonettes cook for 5 minutes, and then drain them in a colander. Discard the cooking oil. The potatoes will be cooked in 10 minutes. Drain them in the same colander as the sole. This operation can be carried out an hour or more before the dish is to be finished and served, leaving you free to have a drink or to enjoy the first course of the meal.

Finishing the dish
6 Heat 30 g (1 oz) butter in a clean frying-pan until it rises into a pale golden foam and then clears. Put the goujonettes and the potatoes in the pan, and then add the pieces of artichoke (1). Season with salt and pepper – none should have been added before this moment. Let everything sizzle in the pan for 3 minutes, stirring carefully with a wooden spatula to avoid breaking the pieces of sole. Sprinkle with the juice of a lemon, add the chopped parsley and serve – fast.

✳ The fillets of sole can be replaced by fillets of John Dory or monkfish, treated in exactly the same way.

✳ There is nothing very new about this recipe; it features in the culinary classics as 'Goujonettes de sole Murat'. But I wanted to bring it to your notice, partly because it is so simple to make and partly for its pleasant fresh quality.

Paul's Baked Pike
Le brochet de mon ami Paul

For two people	Fairly simple
	Moderately expensive
	Preparation time: 50 minutes

Ingredients	1 pike of 1.2 kg (2 lb 10½ oz)
	16 plump unpeeled cloves of garlic (or, if you are a real enthusiast, up to 24)
	50 g (1½ oz) butter
	120 ml (scant ¼ pint) white wine vinegar
	1 small sprig thyme
	salt, pepper

Recommended wines	very light, very young dry white wines such as Beaujolais blanc, Saint-Véran, Côtes du Rhône blanc

✳ It was my friend Paul Bocuse who showed me how to prepare this dish one evening when we were dining together, brother chefs and friends. He and I have the same ideas about cooking and friendship: both should be simple and honest.

✳ Pike can be replaced in this recipe by a sea-fish such as monkfish or various kinds of bream. When perfectly fresh, their eyes and scales should be brilliantly shiny and their bodies so rigid that you can hold them horizontally by the tail and they won't flop.

1 Preheat the oven to 200°C/400°F/Mark 6.

2 If the fishmonger has not already done so, clean and scale the pike. Cut off all the fins. Wash under plenty of cold water and wipe dry with a towel. Season inside and out with salt and pepper. Slide the sprig of thyme into the cavity.

3 Butter an oven-proof oval gratin dish and strew the whole, un-peeled, cloves of garlic in it, and put the pike on top. Spread the remaining butter over the pike and place the dish in the oven. Baste the fish every 5 minutes, making certain that the butter does not burn. If it begins to sizzle, stand the dish inside another, larger, ovenproof dish, or on a baking-sheet, to isolate it a little from the heat. After 15 minutes, add 3 tablespoons of wine vinegar; add another three tablespoons of vinegar every 5 minutes (9 spoonfuls in all) until the pike is cooked. The butter and vinegar will together give the pike a glossy coating and a fine golden colour. The cloves of garlic will be tender and the sauce will have a syrupy consistency, owing to the blending of the butter, which will not have cooked at this temperature, with the vinegar which is considerably reduced. Serve the pike just as it is, in its dish.

Meat

Fricassee of Kidneys and Sweetbreads with Spinach

Fricassée de rognons et de ris de veau aux feuilles d'épinards

For two to three people	Fairly simple
	Expensive
	Preparation time: 20 minutes
	Cooking and finishing time: 15 minutes

Ingredients
1 good quality pale veal kidney
1 set of veal sweetbreads
300 g (10½ oz) leaf spinach
35 g (1¼ oz) butter
1 tablespoon arachide oil
1 shallot, finely chopped
6 generous tablespoons dry white wine
½ chicken stock cube
1 pinch paprika
200 ml (⅓ pint) whipping cream
salt, pepper

Recommended wines   white Burgundy or Pouilly-Fuissé

1 Remove the stalks from the spinach and wash thoroughly in several waters. Drain and place in a medium-sized saucepan containing a tumblerful of fast-boiling salted water. The spinach will wilt as the water returns to the boil; remove it with a slotted spoon and refresh under cold running water, then drain. (Like all green vegetables spinach should be cooked uncovered and refreshed in cold water to keep its natural green colour).

2 Remove the fat, then skin the kidney and cut it into walnut-sized pieces. Put the sweetbreads into 1 litre (1¾ pints) unsalted cold water and bring slowly to simmering point. Simmer for 5 minutes then refresh under cold running water and drain. Remove the gelatinous membranes and any fatty bits carefully. Cut into walnut-sized pieces. Season both kidneys and sweetbreads with salt and pepper.

3 Squeeze the remaining water from the spinach with your hands. Heat 15 g ($\frac{1}{2}$ oz) of butter in a saucepan until the foam has subsided, put in the spinach and stir well with a fork. Season with salt and pepper and keep hot.

4 Heat a nut of butter in a frying-pan, and when the foam begins to subside put in the seasoned sweetbreads and let them cook for 6 minutes, allowing them to turn pale golden. While they are cooking, heat a nut of butter and a trickle of oil in a frying-pan, and when it begins to brown throw in the seasoned kidneys (take care that you don't get splashed with spitting fat). Sauté the pieces of kidney for 3–4 minutes. Then drain both the sweetbreads and the kidneys and keep hot in a colander.

5 Put the dry white wine, together with the chopped shallot, into the pan in which the kidneys have cooked. Reduce over the heat until no more than 2 tablespoons remain. Add the half chicken stock cube crumbled up, a good pinch of paprika and the cream, and simmer for 5 minutes. Adjust the seasoning if necessary. The sauce should be just thick enough to coat the back of a wooden spoon lightly.

6 Put the spinach leaves (1) in the middle of two or three hot plates, spread them out a little and surround them with alternate pieces of kidney and sweetbread. Strain the sauce through a fine sieve and pour it over each piece of kidney and sweetbread, but not the spinach. Serve very hot, and hand any extra sauce separately.

✳ This is not a difficult dish to prepare. Steps (1) and (2) can be carried out a little in advance, leaving only steps (3)–(6) – the actual cooking of the ingredients – to the last moment, when it will take only about 15 minutes to sauté the kidneys and sweetbreads and to finish the sauce.

Kidneys as Cooked at the Moulin de Mougins

Rognons de veau du Moulin

For two people Fairly simple
Fairly expensive
Preparation time: 20 minutes
Cooking time: 20 minutes

Ingredients 2 veal kidneys – to ensure good quality the flesh should be rosy and they should be robed generously in dry white fat
5 tablespoons double cream
30 g (1 oz) butter
1 level tablespoon Dijon mustard
2 tablespoons chopped shallots
3 generous tablespoons Calvados
2 tablespoons coarsely-chopped chervil
salt, pepper

Recommended wines dry white wines, such as white Mâcon, Sancerre

1 Remove all the fat and the skin from the kidneys, leaving them a shining rosy pink. Split each in two lengthways, starting from the edge where the fatty casing was attached. Remove as many of the little tubes, fibres and fatty particles from the interior of the kidneys as you can without destroying their shape. Then, perpendicular to the first cut, slice them in $\frac{1}{2}$ cm ($\frac{1}{4}$ inch) thick rounds – about the size of a French five-franc piece, an English fifty-pence piece or an Australian fifty-cent piece. Put the pieces on a plate and season well with salt and pepper.

2 In a shallow pan with sloping sides heat half the butter over a fierce heat. When the foam subsides put in half the seasoned kidneys. Let them sear throughly then turn them with a wooden spatula. They should be cooked in 4–5 minutes. Drain the kidneys in a colander placed over a bowl to catch the juices and blood that will run out. Repeat the operation, using the remaining butter to cook the rest of the kidneys, and when they are cooked add them to the first batch in the colander. Keep hot.

3 Now add the chopped shallots to the cooking juices in the pan, pour in the Calvados and scrape up the butter and juices with the wooden spatula. Don't let the Calvados catch fire – that's not the object of the exercise. When the shallot has softened in the juices and the Calvados, add the cream and boil for 2–3 minutes, whisking all the time.

4 Strain the sauce through a fine sieve placed over a clean saucepan, working it through with the spatula. Add the Dijon mustard and whisk again to mix it in thoroughly. Put the kidneys (2) into the sauce and heat through to just below boiling point. Taste for seasoning, add the chopped chervil and serve on hot plates.

✳ It is vital not to boil kidneys as they acquire the texture of rubber.

Calves' Liver with Radishes and Turnips

Aiguillettes de foie de veau aux radis et aux navets

For two people	Fairly simple
	Fairly expensive
	Preparation time: soaking the liver 1 hour
	Cooking time: 45 minutes

Ingredients	2 slices of calves' liver of 180 g (6½ oz) each
	75 g (2½ oz) butter
	150 g (5½ oz) small tender turnips
	16 radishes of equal shape and size
	1 tablespoon chopped onion
	200 ml (⅓ pint) milk
	50 g (1¾ oz) flour
	3 tablespoons wine vinegar
	1 teaspoon Dijon mustard
	3 tablespoons stock made with a beef stock cube
	1 tablespoon chopped parsley
	salt, pepper

Recommended wines	red, such as Saint-Emilion, Saint-Estèphe or Coteaux d'Aix

1 Lay the slices of liver on the chopping board and slice into strips the thickness of your little finger. Put the strips in a bowl containing the milk and mix well with your hands. Put in a cool place for 1 hour. The object of this operation is to draw out the blood and make the meat more tender. When the hour is up, drain in a colander and discard the milk, unless you have a cat.

2 Peel the turnips and cut them into little sticks about 2 cm ($\frac{3}{4}$ inch) by 5 mm ($\frac{1}{4}$ inch). Put them in a saucepan with a nut of butter and just enough water to cover them. Add a pinch of salt, and cook until the water has totally evaporated: the turnips should still be white and slightly firm.

3 Cut off the root and most of the leaves of the radishes, keeping a little tuft of stalks 2 cm ($\frac{3}{4}$ inch) long. Wash and drain them. Melt a nut of butter in a small saucepan and when it begins to foam throw in the radishes, salt lightly and cook over a low heat for 2–3 minutes. Then put them to keep hot in the same saucepan as the turnips.

4 Put a nut of butter and a tablespoon of chopped onion into the saucepan in which the radishes were cooked. Allow to brown lightly over a moderate heat then add the vinegar and reduce to 1 tablespoon of liquid. Add the beef stock and cook gently, covered, for 5 minutes without reducing. Put the pan and its contents on one side to keep hot.

5 Put the flour in a plate and throw in the strips of liver, well salted and peppered. Mix them around well so that each strip is lightly coated in flour. Then, one by one, place the slices on the working surface and roll them with the flat of your hand. Heat a heaped tablespoon of butter in a large frying pan and when it ceases to sizzle put in the floured and seasoned liver, turning the pieces over so that they cook evenly. Make sure they do not overcook, and are still rosy inside. Drain in a carefully dried colander and keep hot. Wipe the pan, but do not wash it.

6 Return the saucepan containing the sauce (4) to the heat and beat in, bit by bit, 40 g (1$\frac{1}{2}$ oz) butter cut into little pieces. Do not let it boil and remove the pan from the heat when the butter is all incorporated. Add the Dijon mustard and taste for seasoning. Strain the sauce through a fine sieve into the frying-pan. Add the cooked liver (5) and the chopped parsley. Bring almost to the boil, coating all the pieces of liver generously with the sauce. Divide between two hot plates and surround the liver with the hot turnips and radishes (3).

Jamaican Pork Fricassee

Fricassée de grouet Jamaïquain

For two people	Fairly simple
	Moderately expensive
	Preparation time: 20 minutes
	Cooking time: 1 hour 20 minutes

Ingredients	2 pork chops weighing 250 g (9 oz) each
	2 ripe tomatoes weighing 90–100 g (3¼–3½ oz) each
	1 medium onion weighing about 120 g (4½ oz)
	1 clove garlic
	1 bouquet garni made up of 1 sprig of thyme, 1 bayleaf, 2 sprigs parsley and a small piece of celery, tied with a thread
	½ stick of cinnamon
	a pinch of nutmeg
	1 banana
	2 tablespoons flour
	3 tablespoons dry white wine
	2 tablespoons olive oil
	20 g (¾ oz) butter
	salt, pepper

Recommended wines	Sturdy red wines (Brouilly, Moulin à Vent or Coteaux d'Aix)

✸ This dish was something of a problem to me, because when I christened it 'Fricassée de porc jamaïquain' I found that a lot of customers – wrongly, since it is a most delicious meat – dislike pork. I was rather depressed by the dish's lack of success, so I renamed it, using the Swahili word for pork, 'grouet', which I had learned in East Africa. Thus embellished with a mixture of African folklore and West Indian romance it immediately became a favourite dish. Unfortunately, at that time I had a head waiter who was incapable of lying (they do exist). Asked by a customer what exactly 'grouet' was, he fled, muttering 'Oh, I think perhaps it's a kind of veal.' Honour was (almost) saved and the happy customer thoroughly enjoyed his meal.

1 Preheat the oven to 150°C/300°F/Mark 2. Peel the onion and slice into fine rounds. Peel the garlic and chop it coarsely. Bring 1 litre (1¾ pints) of water to the boil and plunge in the tomatoes. After 1 minute remove them and refresh under cold running water. Peel the tomatoes and cut them in half horizontally. Press each half in the palm of your hand to squeeze out seeds and excess moisture and chop the flesh coarsely.

2 Heat the olive oil in a large enamelled cast-iron casserole. Meanwhile, season the pork chops with salt and pepper, and sprinkle lightly with flour. When the oil is hot, sear the chops. Let them turn pearly white on both sides, then remove them and keep aside on a plate. Throw the onion slices into the hot casserole and fry to a beautiful golden colour, then add the garlic and the bouquet garni. Lay the pork chops on the bed of onion, scatter the diced tomatoes over the top and add the cinnamon and nutmeg. Pour in the white wine, cover and cook in the oven for 1¼ hours. Watch to see that the cooking liquid doesn't evaporate too quickly (which may happen if the lid is loose). If it does, add 2 tablespoons of water.

3 A few minutes before the end of the cooking, peel the banana. Cut it in half lengthways and then cut each piece in half. Sprinkle each of the these four pieces with flour. Heat the butter in a small frying-pan and brown the pieces of banana. They should still be slightly firm. Drain on a plate and keep warm.

4 When 1¼ hours are up, make sure that the pork is thoroughly cooked. The vegetables should have reduced to a thick purée; if not, cook for a little longer. Remove the bouquet garni and the cinnamon. Place a pork chop on each of two heated plates and pour over the sauce, well seasoned with salt and pepper. Decorate each chop with two pieces of banana. Serve with plain boiled rice.

Rib of Beef with Shallots and Vinegar

Côte de boeuf aux échalotes et au vinaigre

For two people	Simple Moderately expensive *Cooking time:* 30 minutes
Ingredients	1 rib of beef weighing 800–1000 g (1 lb 12 oz–2¼ lb) 3 finely-chopped shallots 2 tablespoons wine vinegar 2 tablespoons chopped parsley 70 g (2½ oz) butter salt, pepper
Recommended wines	Light red wines (new Beaujolais or fairly young Saint-Estèphe)

✳ Professional chefs judge the cooking of meat by touch, that is by pressing their index and middle fingers into the centre of the meat. If it is soft the meat is very rare, or 'bleu'; if it is firm on the outside but supple inside, the meat is rare or 'saignant' and when the pressure of the fingers produces a drop of pink juice the meat is well done or 'à point'. I would always advise you to cook your meat rare or 'saignant' as it has more flavour. It is always best to leave red meat (grilled, fried or roasted) to rest for 10 minutes before serving. This allows the blood to become stabilised. Otherwise it runs out when it is cut.

1 Season the beef with salt and pepper on both sides, and rub in the seasoning with the tips of your fingers.

2 Heat a generous tablespoon of butter in a frying-pan and when it begins to foam put in the beef. Lower the heat so that the meat does not acquire a hard crust, and cook for 5–10 minutes each side, depending on the thickness of the meat and how well done you want it. Take care that the butter does not burn.

3 Remove the meat and keep it hot. To do this put it on an upturned plate placed inside a larger one, and cover the whole thing with an upturned bowl. This allows the meat to rest without drowning in its own juices, which would spoil the texture.

4 Pour away the cooking butter and replace it with the remaining butter, together with the chopped shallots. Return to a medium heat and allow to soften for 5 minutes, without allowing the shallots to brown. Add the wine vinegar and cook for a further 5 minutes, stirring with a wooden spoon. Season with a few turns of the peppermill and salt if needed. Add the chopped parsley and the juices which have run out of the meat (3). Mix well with a wooden spoon and pour into a sauceboat. Keep hot.

5 Cut the beef in thick slices, giving each person an equal quantity of lean and fat. Serve very hot, accompanied by the shallot sauce. This dish is especially popular with meat-lovers and needs only a salad of curly endive seasoned with a mustardy vinaigrette. And if the accompanying wine is cool and fresh I promise you a splendid meal.

Fillet of Beef with Currants Mathurini
Filet de boeuf aux raisins à la mathurini

For two people	Simple
	Very expensive
	Cooking time: 25 minutes

Ingredients	2 trimmed slices of fillet (**or** contre-filet) weighing 180–200 g (6½–7 oz) each
	40 g (1½ oz) currants
	1 tablespoon coarsely crushed black pepper (crush it in a pestle and mortar or wrap in a cloth and crush with a bottle)
	50 g (1¾ oz) butter
	3 tablespoons armagnac **or** cognac
	3 tablespoons stock made with ½ beef stock cube
	salt

Recommended wines	Coteaux d'Aix, Bandol, Côtes du Rhône or other full-bodied red wine

✳ Why 'à la mathurini'? The first time I made it I served it with maize pancakes and a few leaves of spinach cooked in butter. The spinach reminded me of Popeye, but I thought that would be too frivolous. Then I remembered Popeye's friend Mathurin, and from Mathurin to mathurini was only a short step. Incidentally, spinach harmonises exceedingly well with this dish.

1 Bring ½ litre (scant pint) water to the boil and throw in the currants. Allow to boil for 5 minutes, then drain and refresh under cold water.

2 Salt the beef on both sides and roll in the crushed pepper, pressing it well into the meat with the flat of your hand.

3 Heat a little of the butter in a small frying-pan and cook the fillets, allowing 2–3 minutes on each side over a moderate heat. (The cooking time is only a suggestion, much depends on the thickness and texture of the meat and on your own taste. A note on this subject can be found in the previous recipe.) When they are cooked, remove the steaks and keep them hot on an upturned plate placed on a larger one and covered with a bowl. This allows the meat to keep hot without drowning in its own juices.

4 Pour off the butter in which the steaks have been cooked but do not wash the pan. Put the currants in the pan with the armagnac or cognac *away from the heat* (because the object of using spirit is to loosen the meat juices from the surface of the pan, and not to perform a firework display). Reduce over a low heat, then add the stock. Simmer for 2 minutes without allowing the liquid to reduce too much. Then gradually add the remaining butter in small pieces, giving the pan four or five swirling shakes to incorporate the butter into the sauce, without giving it a chance to become 'oily'. Add salt if necessary.

5 Arrange the steaks on two hot plates and pour the sauce over them.

Medallions of Veal with Lemon

Les filets mignons de veau au citron

For two people   Fairly simple
Fairly expensive
Cooking time: 1 hour

Ingredients   300 g (10½ oz) veal fillet (tenderloin) cut into 4
pieces and trimmed of fat and sinews **or** 2
first grade veal cutlets trimmed of their fat
1 ripe juicy lemon
60 g (2 oz) butter
4 tablespoons dry white wine
1 tablespoon chopped parsley
½ teaspoon sugar
salt, pepper

1 Pare off the peel of half the lemon as thinly as possible with a potato-peeler and cut into thin julienne strips. Put the strips of peel in a small pan with cold water and bring to the boil. Drain and refresh under the cold tap. Return the blanched peel to the pan with half a teaspoon of sugar and 1 tablespoon of water and cook until the water has evaporated and the peel has become a beautiful bright yellow. Remove from the heat and keep on one side.

2 Heat a third of the butter in a frying-pan, and meanwhile season the pieces of veal on both sides with salt and pepper. When the butter begins to sizzle, cook the veal over a moderate heat, giving it about 5 minutes on each side. Remove the meat and keep hot. Pour away the cooking butter but not wash the pan. Deglaze the pan with the white wine over a moderate heat, scraping up the caramelized juices from the bottom of the pan and allowing the wine to reduce until there is only a generous tablespoonful left. Then add the remaining butter and mix very well to amalgamate the sauce. Add the chopped parsley, taste and season with salt and pepper.

3 Arrange the veal on two hot plates and add the juices which have run out of it to the sauce. Pour the sauce – there will be very little of it – over the meat and decorate each medallion with a slice of peeled lemon and a pinch of the cooked julienne of lemon peel (1).

✳ Risotto or fresh young vegetables cooked in butter are good with this dish.

Roast Best End of Lamb with Green Peppercorns
Carré d'agneau rôti au poivre vert

For two people Fairly simple
Rather expensive
Preparation time: 25 minutes
Cooking time: 10 minutes

Ingredients 1 best end of lamb weighing 800 g (1 lb 12 oz). Ask your butcher for the loin end of a best end containing about 7 cutlets and get him to prepare it ready for roasting and to give you the bones and any pieces he trims away.
20 g (⅔ oz) butter
20 g (⅔ oz) green peppercorns
30 g (1 oz) sieved breadcrumbs
2 teaspoons strong mustard
1 egg white
1 tablespoon chopped parsley
salt, pepper

Recommended wines Full-bodied red wine (Saint-Emilion, Coteaux d'Aix)

❋ Served like this with a few French beans dressed with butter this cut of lamb, usually considered modest enough, becomes a dish of some character.

1 Preheat the oven to the hottest possible setting. Allow it at least 15 minutes to heat up.

2 Place the meat in a roasting-dish, season it with salt and pepper and arrange the trimmings and bones round it, coating it with half the butter. Roast for 20 minutes in the very hot oven, basting from time to time.

3 When the meat is cooked, let it rest for five or so minutes on an upturned plate placed on another larger one and covered with a bowl (this allows the meat to keep hot without drowning in its own juices, which would spoil the texture).

4 While the meat is cooking, crush the green peppercorns and mix them with the parsley and mustard. Whisk the egg white until it is very firm, then fold in the green pepper mixture.

5 Pour the cooking fat from the roasting-dish and keep it hot. Deglaze the dish with 3–4 tablespoons of water, stirring the bones well to extract all the juices. Strain the resulting sauce into a small saucepan, add a turn of the peppermill and the remaining butter.

6 Turn the grill to its highest setting and, while it heats up, spread a thick layer of the egg and green pepper mixture (4) 1 cm ($\frac{1}{4}$ inch) thick on the upper side of the meat. Sprinkle with breadcrumbs and then baste with some of the fat from the roasting-dish (5). Place the meat carefully in the roasting-dish, on top of the bones, and grill 3–4 minutes until it has turned a pretty golden colour. Serve at once, with the sauce (5) in a separate sauceboat.

✱ To whisk egg whites really successfully you must make sure that the bowl is completely free of grease by rubbing it with a piece of lemon and rinsing it in fresh water. Dry it thoroughly and before you start to whisk the egg whites, add a pinch of salt, and make certain they are not too cold.

Lamb Estouffade with Garlic Bread

Estouffade de gigot d'agneau avec les tartines d'ail

For six or seven people	Fairly simple Fairly cheap *Preparation time:* 1 hour *Marinade:* 4 hours *Cooking time:* 3¼ hours

Ingredients	1 leg of lamb weighing 3 kg (6½ lb), boned by the butcher 400 g (14 oz) salt belly of pork, soaked and cut in strips the size of your thumb 300 g (10½ oz) salt pork rind 2 bottles – 1·5 litres (2½ pints) full bodied red wine 240 g (8¾ oz) coarsely-chopped onion 4 cloves of garlic, peeled and flattened 4 tomatoes weighing 100 g (3½ oz) each 2 beef stock cubes 1 bouquet garni made up of parsley, celery, a bayleaf, a strip of orange peel and 2 sprigs of thyme tied up with a thread 3 tablespoons olive oil 200 g (7 oz) flour salt 1 tablespoon crushed black peppercorns

Recommended wines	Full-bodied red wines (Bandol, Coteaux d'Aix, Cornas or Saint-Joseph Côtes du Rhône)

1 Trim the leg of lamb and cut the meat into large chunks weighing 80–90 g (about 3 oz) each. Put them in a large enamelled cast-iron casserole, together with the chopped onions, peeled and flattened cloves of garlic, peeled, deseeded and diced tomatoes, the bouquet garni and the crushed peppercorns. Pour in the red wine and the olive oil and mix thoroughly with a wooden spoon. Set aside in a cool place (but not in the refrigerator) to marinate for 4 hours.

2 Meanwhile, cut the pork skin into 2 cm (1 inch) squares and place in a large pan full of cold water together with the strips of belly. Bring to the boil and simmer for 5 minutes, then drain and refresh under the cold tap.

3 When the meat has been marinating for 3½ hours, preheat the oven to 110°C/225°F/Mark ¼. Half an hour later when the meat has marinated for 4 hours add the drained pork (2) to the casserole together with the stock cubes. Stir well and season with 2 teaspoons coarse salt. Add enough cold water to bring the level of the marinade 2 cm (1 inch) above the meat, and cover the casserole. Mix the flour with cold water in a bowl and seal the casserole with the resulting paste. Put the sealed casserole in the oven and forget about it for 3 hours.

4 To serve, you have only to remove the sealing crust, throw away the bouquet garni, remove any excess fat with a spoon and taste for seasoning. The stew should be served very hot, in soup plates, with garlic bread made in the following way.

Garlic Bread
Les tartines d'ail doux

For six or seven people
5 whole heads garlic
3 tablespoons olive oil
a French 'baguette' loaf
salt

1 Take five whole heads of garlic and separate them. If the garlic is sprouting vigorously, cut each clove in half and remove the green part. Boil the peeled cloves in 2 litres of salted water for 5 minutes. Drain in a sieve and repeat 3 times, starting with fresh water each time. Leave the garlic to simmer in the final lot of water until it is cooked and soft. Then drain the garlic and purée in the liquidiser or sieve through the fine blade of the mouli-légumes. Mix the garlic puree with the olive oil and season with salt.

2 Cut the 'baguette' loaf into about thirty little slices and grill them on both sides, spread with the garlic purée and grill lightly. Serve with the Estouffade, dipping them in the juices … and you will see the point.

Lamb Stew with Beans and Lambs' Trotters

Blanquette d'agneau aux haricots et aux pieds d'agneau

For five or six people

Fairly simple
Fairly cheap
Preparation time: soaking the beans 12 hours
Cooking time: 3½ hours

Ingredients

1·5 kg (3¼ lb) boned shoulder of lamb
3 lambs' trotters
400 g (14 oz) dried 'flageolet' beans
2 onions
1 leek
1–2 cloves
6 carrots
3 little bouquets garnis, each made up of a sprig of thyme, 4 sprigs of parsley, a small stick of celery and a bayleaf tied with a thread
1 tablespoon flour
20 g (⅔ oz) peppercorns
2 lemons
1 beef stock cube
3 tablespoons Dijon mustard
300 ml (½ pint) double cream
4 egg yolks
1 tablespoon chopped parsley
1 tablespoon chopped chervil
salt, pepper

Recommended wines

Red Bordeaux (Saint-Emilion or Saint-Estèphe)

Twelve hours in advance
1 Soak the beans in plenty of cold water.

2 Trim as much fat as possible and cut the meat into large chunks, each one weighing about 40–50 g (about 1½ oz). Put the chunks into a bowl of iced water and chill in the refrigerator for 12 hours, changing the water once or twice. This process draws the blood out of the meat and whitens it.

Cooking the dish
3 Drain the soaked beans and cook in 3 litres (5¼ pints) cold water with one of the onions stuck with one or two cloves, 2 carrots, the leek and 1 bouquet garni. Allow to cook gently over a moderate heat for 2 hours. Skim frequently and add salt after ¼ hour. The cooking time will vary according to the quality and age of the beans, so try one from time to time.

4 While the beans are cooking, rub the lambs' trotters with lemon juice and plunge them into 3 litres (5¼ pints) of boiling water. Simmer for 10 minutes to blanch or 'scald' them and then refresh under the cold tap. Remove the hooves and put the feet to cook in 3 litres (5¼ pints) cold water to which you have added the juice of a lemon and a tablespoon of flour, first mixed to a thin cream with water, 2 carrots, a bouquet garni and a few peppercorns. Cook for about 2 hours (but take care not to overcook them).

5 While the beans and lambs' trotters are cooking, drain the pieces of lamb and put them to cook in a saucepan with 3 litres (5¼ pints) cold water to which you have added 1 stock cube, 2 whole peeled carrots, 1 whole onion, a few peppercorns and a bouquet garni. Add a little salt and cook over a moderate heat for 1½ hours.

6 When the lambs' trotters are cooked, drain them and allow to cool. Then skin them completely, remove the bones and cut into fairly large pieces.

7 When they are cooked, drain the pieces of lamb (5) and reduce their cooking liquid over a brisk heat until you have only 1 litre (1¾ pints) left. Put the lamb and the chopped lambs' trotters (6)
(continued on the next page)

into a flame-proof earthenware casserole and keep hot while you make the sauce.

8 Mix the cream, Dijon mustard and egg yolks in a bowl and add the reduced cooking liquid from the lamb (7). Whisk thoroughly and pour the mixture into a saucepan. Heat very gently, whisking all the time and adding salt and pepper. Just before the sauce comes to the boil, remove from the heat and strain through a fine wire sieve over the pieces of lamb in the casserole. Drain the beans – which should be very hot – remove the various vegetables with which they have cooked and fold them into the blanquette. Heat them through, briefly, sprinkle with chopped parsley and chervil, and serve.

✳ You can replace the flageolet beans in this dish with other kinds of dried beans, or even with fresh white haricot beans. But as this is really a dish for winter I prefer to use dried beans. If you do use fresh haricots allow 1 kg (2¼ lb) of shelled beans. They won't need soaking and they need only be cooked for 30 minutes.

Poultry
and Game

Chicken in Salt

Poulet sous la croûte au sel

For three to *four people*	Fairly simple Fairly inexpensive *Preparation time:* 30 minutes *Cooking time:* 1 hour 30 minutes

Ingredients 1 fresh white-fleshed farm chicken of 1·8 kg (4 lb)
3 chicken livers
1 kg (2¼ lb) coarse sea salt
1 kg (2¼ lb) flour
1 sprig rosemary
1 bayleaf
salt, pepper
curly endive
wine vinegar, walnut oil

Recommended *wines* young fresh red wines such as Beaujolais, Côtes de Provence

1 Preheat the oven to 150°C/300°F/Mark 2. Mix the salt and the flour in a large bowl, together with 6 tablespoons of cold water. Knead till you have a homogeneous paste and then spread out on a lightly floured work-top with the palm of your hand. Season the inside (only the inside) of the chicken with salt and pepper and slide in the rosemary, the bayleaf and washed chicken livers. Wrap the chicken in the salt/flour paste, making sure that it is hermetically sealed, and place it in a shallow oven-proof dish. Place in the oven and cook for 1½ hours.

2 Near the end of the cooking time, make a green salad with the endive and season with a good vinaigrette made of wine vinegar and walnut oil (1 tablespoon of wine vinegar to 4 of oil).

3 Put the chicken in its crust on a chopping board and take it to the table. In front of your guests, cut off the top of the crust with a strong knife – be careful, it will be extremely hard. Remove the chicken to a warm serving dish and carve it. Remove the chicken livers from the interior, chop them coarsely and mix them into the salad. The chicken, which has cooked in steam inside the crust, retains all its own flavour, tinged just a little with aromas of rosemary and bay.

✱ You can prepare this dish in advance as it will keep perfectly well in its crust for 30–40 minutes, but in that case cook it for only 1 hour and 15 minutes and leave the crust intact until you serve it. During the fresh truffle season you could slide 2 handsome truffles of about 50 g (1½ oz) each inside the chicken before encasing it in paste. You will find that the result isn't altogether unpleasing.

Grilled Chicken with Lemon

Poulet grillé au citron

For two people	Fairly simple
	Fairly inexpensive
	Preparation time: 20 minutes
	Marination time: 4 hours
	Cooking time: 35 minutes

Ingredients
1 white-fleshed chicken, of 1·4 kg (3 lb) plucked, cleaned and singed
1 onion of 120 g (4¼ oz), preferably a young one
2 large handsome lemons
1 teaspoon of oregano
5 tablespoons of olive oil
salt, pepper

Recommended wines Beaujolais Villages, Bourgueil or red wine from the Coteaux de Nice

✳ A plain tomato salad is the perfect accompaniment for this chicken. To make a good tomato salad, take four firm tomatoes of 120 g (4¼ oz) each. Wash them, remove the stalks and cut each into eight sections. Put in a bowl and season with a tablespoon – yes, a tablespoon – of fine salt. Add pepper, and sprinkle with 4 tablespoons of wine vinegar and 2 tablespoons of olive oil. Mix well and leave to rest for 2–3 hours. Just before serving, drain the tomatoes in a colander and throw away the juice. Sprinkle the drained tomatoes with 3 tablespoons olive oil and strew with 1 tablespoon of chopped parsley.

Five hours in advance
1 Remove the feet, the neck and the wing tips of the chicken, and stand it on its back on a chopping-board. Split in half with a large heavy knife, cutting alongside the vertebral column. Remove the backbone completely by making a second cut parallel to the first. Make a small incision through the ball and socket joint where the drumsticks meet the thighs. Flatten each half of the chicken by smacking it with the flat of a cleaver – but don't squash it!

2 Season the chicken on both sides with salt and pepper and sprinkle all over with oregano. Peel the onion and cut into fine slices. Spread them over the bottom of an enamelled iron gratin dish and lay the chicken, skin-side up, on this bed of onions. Slice one of the lemons into very fine rounds and arrange them over the chicken. Sprinkle with 2 tablespoons of olive oil. Cover the roasting tin with a sheet of aluminium foil and leave to marinate for 4 hours, not in the refrigerator.

Cooking the dish
3 Heat the grill to its highest setting. Preheat the oven to 250°C/ 500°F/Mark 10. Remove the chicken from the marinade (2) and put the slices of lemon on one side. Put the chicken in a roasting-tin and grill until it is a beautiful golden brown. Then turn the pieces over, sprinkle with a tablespoon of olive oil and brown the other side. When the chicken is nicely browned put it back on top of the onions in the gratin dish in which it marinated, skin side up. Replace the slices of lemon. Sprinkle with 2 tablespoons olive oil, roast in the oven for 25 minutes. After 15 minutes, sprinkle the chicken with the juice of the second lemon.

4 When the chicken is cooked, remove and cut each half in two. Return to the gratin dish, place on the onion bed and spoon the cooking juices over it. Serve very hot.

Duck Cooked in Wine with Apples and Prunes

Canard en civet au vieux vin et aux fruits

For two people	Fairly simple
	Moderately expensive
	Preparation time: marination, 12 hours
	Cooking and finishing the dish: 2 hours

Ingredients

1 duck of 2–2.5 kg (4½–5½ lb)

1 bottle 750 ml (1¼ pints) strong, very full-bodied Burgundy, Côtes du Rhône or Algerian red wine

1 small stick celery

1 carrot

1 onion

3 cloves of garlic

30 g (1 oz) butter

2 tablespoons flour

1 Golden Delicious apple

10 half walnuts

10 stoned prunes

a little muslin bag containing: 10 black peppercorns, 1 clove, 4 juniper berries, a sprig of thyme, a strip of orange peel, 1 bayleaf, 4 sprigs of parsley. Tie the muslin up round the four corners with a piece of cotton without squeezing up the contents too much so that they can swell and give out their flavours.

Recommended wines	solid red wines – Pommard, Côte-Rôtie, Bandol

One day in advance

1 Singe and clean the duck and cut it up in the following way. Cut off and discard the head and feet. Cut off the wings and neck and put them on one side. Detach the legs and the two breasts and chop the remainder of the carcass into small pieces, together with the neck and wings, using a heavy knife or cleaver. Put everything in a large bowl.

2 Peel the carrot, garlic and onion and trim the celery, and cut them all into fine slices which are then strewn over the pieces of duck. Bury the little bag of aromatics in the middle and pour over the bottle of wine. Cover the bowl and leave to marinate in a cool place (but not in the refrigerator) for 10–12 hours (but not more than 18 hours). At the same time, put the prunes to soak in warm water for the same period.

Cooking and finishing the dish

3 Drain the duck and all the vegetables in a colander placed over a large saucepan. Drain the prunes and add them to the strained marinade, together with the nuts and the little bag of aromatics. Simmer gently for 15 minutes.

4 Meanwhile, heat 15 g ($\frac{1}{2}$ oz) butter in a large enamelled cast-iron casserole. Dry the legs and breasts of the duck carefully, and season them with salt and pepper all over. When the butter starts to sizzle, put in the pieces of duck, skin-side down. Let them brown gently so that the fat runs out of the duck skin, and then turn the pieces over to allow the flesh side to brown. Remove them to a plate, and put the crushed carcass, neck and wings and the vegetables (1) into the casserole. Let them brown, then drain off the fat from the casserole by tilting it over a basin with the lid just slightly askew. Return the casserole to the heat, sprinkle the contents with 2 tablespoons flour and stir well for 2–3 minutes. Replace the duck breasts and legs on top of the bones and vegetables and pour on the marinade (3) through a fine wire strainer. Keep the prunes and walnut halves on one side and discard the bag of aromatics. If the liquid does not cover the duck completely, add a little warm water. Simmer very gently for 45 minutes, covered, over a very low heat.

(*continued on the next page*)

5 At the end of this time, make certain the pieces of duck are cooked by piercing the drumstick with a fork, which should meet with no resistance. Put the pieces of duck on a plate with the prunes and nuts and keep warm. Remove the casserole from the heat, and prop it up on a fork or other small object so that it is at an angle. This is to enable the fat to rise to the top of the sauce, so that after a few minutes it can be easily removed with a spoon.

6 While the sauce is resting, peel the apple, cut it in half, remove the pips and core and cut into little cubes. Heat 15 g ($\frac{1}{2}$ oz) butter in a frying-pan, and when the butter ceases to sizzle put in the apple cubes. Cook until golden, then drain and add to the duck.

7 Remove the fat from the top of the sauce (5) and return the casserole to the heat, reducing the liquid until there is only a tumbler left. Sieve the sauce through a fine wire strainer into a saucepan. Throw out the bones and vegetables, clean the casserole and place the duck pieces, prunes, nuts and apple cubes in it. Taste the sauce, and season with salt and freshly-ground pepper. Pour it over the duck in the casserole, bring to the boil, simmer for 5–10 minutes and serve just as it is.

✳ This dish can easily be reheated.

✳ Our grandparents used to cook duck in this way and I have simply embellished it by adding the fruit. The 'Nouvelle Cuisine' isn't a matter of re-inventing everything and despising traditional methods. On the contrary, the chefs of today, in spite of the jokes about them, respect and admire the traditional cuisines of the French regions, which use fresh cream, good butter and high quality natural produce. Quite simply we are trying to evolve a saner, healthier cuisine. That is the reason that we don't use flour in our sauces, as was the custom until recently. For flour absorbs fat, which is not easy to digest. In this recipe for stewed duck, there is less than a quarter of the flour which would be used to make a single croissant, but it is enough to bind the sauce without stabilising the fat, which rises to the surface and is easily removed.

Duck as Served at the Moulin de Mougins

Le canard comme au Moulin

For two people	Rather complicated Moderately expensive *Preparation time:* 1½ hours
Ingredients	1 duck of 2·8 kg (6–6¼ lb), plucked and cleaned 250 ml (scant half-pint) full-bodied red wine 40 g (1½ oz) butter 4 coarsely-chopped shallots 1 teaspoon tomato purée 4 juniper berries 1 sprig thyme 1 chicken stock cube 2 tablespoons cognac salt, pepper
Recommended wines	Sturdy red wines: Burgundy (Pommard) Bordeaux (Margaux) or possibly Côtes du Rhône (Côte-Rôtie)

Editor's note

In this and the preceding dish, Roger Vergé recommends ducks that are killed in a special way – by smothering – to conserve their blood. Most cooks outside France, however, will have to be content with ordinary ducks.

1 Preheat the oven to 250°C/500°F/Mark 10. Hold the duck in a gas jet to remove all the remaining stubs of feathers (or use a taper). Remove the feet, wing tips and neck with a large knife. If the duck has not yet been gutted, do so, leaving in the heart, lungs and liver. Place the juniper berries and the thyme inside the duck and season it with salt and pepper, inside and out. Truss it with kitchen string.

2 Put the wing tips and the neck chopped into pieces in a roasting tin just large enough to hold the bird and lay the duck on its side on top. Cover it with 20 g (¾ oz) butter and place it in the hot oven. After 8 minutes, turn the duck over on to the other side, and after a further 8 minutes place it breastside up and cook for a further 10 minutes. This operation sears the duck all over and causes it to shed the excess fat in its skin.

3 Remove the duck and let it rest in a warm place for 10 minutes. Throw out the fat from the roasting tin and pour in the red wine, leaving in the wings and neck. Boil for a few minutes to deglaze the pan of the meat juices. Then put on one side.

4 Remove the legs from the duck, cutting the skin carefully with a sharp knife, and set on one side. Remove the wishbone with the point of a small sharp knife. Skin the duck completely. Then carve five long slices from each breast, working parallel to the backbone (these are called 'aiguillettes'). Keep hot.

5 Take the carcass of the duck and remove the heart, lungs and liver, which should be set aside on a chopping board. Remove the juniper berries and the thyme and add them to the juices in the roasting-tin (3). Chop up the carcass with a heavy knife or cleaver. Heat 20 g (¾ oz) butter in a saucepan and throw in the chopped carcass. Stir the pieces about so that they brown all over. Add the four coarsely-chopped shallots and the tomato purée. Let the shallots brown a little then flame with the cognac. When the flames have died down add the wine from the roasting tin (3), together with the neck and wing tips, and boil till you have no more than a coffeecup of liquid left. Add just enough hot water to cover the bones, and put in the stock cube. Boil for 20 minutes. Meanwhile, chop the heart, lungs and a quarter of the liver finely (keep the

rest for the cat). When the 20 minutes is up, strain the contents of the roasting-tin into another saucepan through a fine wire sieve and then reduce again until no more than a coffeecupful of the liquid remains. Add the chopped heart, lungs and liver, bring to the boil again briefly and strain again, into a bowl. Season with a few turns of the pepper-mill – the sauce should already be salty enough – and keep the sauce hot in a bain-marie.

6 A quarter of an hour or so before you want to eat the dish, season the duck legs on the flesh side with coarse salt and grill for 15 minutes. During this time, divide the sauce between two hot plates and lay five slices of duck (4) on each, making sure they are well bathed in the sauce. Put in the hot oven for a few minutes to heat through and serve. On a second plate, put the grilled duck legs, served simply with a green salad (curly endive or escarole) seasoned with wine vinegar and walnut oil.

✳ This dish can be prepared in the morning up to the point in step (5) where the chopped giblets are about to be added to the sauce. This and the finishing of the dish must be done just before serving. If you do prepare the dish in advance, on no account put the duck legs or slices of breast in the refrigerator.

Fricassee of Chicken with Wine Vinegar
Fricassée de poulet au vinaigre de vin

For four people	Fairly simple Moderately expensive *Preparation time:* 1 hour 20 minutes
Ingredient	1 white-fleshed chicken of 2 kg (4½ lb) cleaned and divided into four pieces 250 ml (scant half-pint) white wine vinegar 250 ml (scant half-pint) red wine 500 g (1 lb 2 oz) yellow onions 2 cloves of garlic 2 ripe tomatoes of 100 g (3½ oz) each a bouquet garni made up of celery, a sprig of thyme, a small bayleaf, a few sprigs of parsley, tied together with a thread 60 g (2 oz) butter
Recommended wines	Beaujolais or red Burgundy (Morgon, Brouilly, Moulin à Vent or Volnay)

✷ This recipe reminds me of something that happened to me when I was in Kenya. One day I was preparing a grand dinner for some English VIP, and I'd ordered chickens from the Allier. The airlines went on strike, as is their wont, and my chickens never arrived. Unfortunately, the menus had already been printed and there was no way of changing the dish. In despair, I dispatched my assistants into the surrounding countryside to conduct a raid for chickens. An hour later, I had dozens ... and dozens, but all as scrawny and muscular as marathon runners. When the time came to cook them they proved to be not only as tough as old boots but as dark-fleshed as game-birds. It was a far cry from my tender poultry from Allier. Never have I had to cook chickens for so long and so repeatedly; finally the gas ran out and I was reduced to breaking up chairs to feed the stoves. And the outcome? The VIP declared that there was nothing to beat an Allier chicken!

1 Peel the onions and cut them in fine rounds. Put them in an ena-melled cast-iron casserole with 15 g (½ oz) butter and 2 tablespoons water. Cover and cook over gentle heat for about 30 minutes, stir-ring from time to time with a wooden spoon to make sure they do not stick and burn. If they start to brown add 2 more table-spoons of water and reduce the heat. While the onions are cooking remove the stalks of the tomatoes, cut them in half horizontally and press with your palm to expel excess moisture and seeds. Chop coarsely into dice. Peel and crush the cloves of garlic. When the onions are cooked, add the tomatoes and cook a further 5 minutes. Then remove from the heat and keep the casserole warm with its lid on, having first buried the bouquet garni and the cloves of garlic in the middle of the onions and tomatoes.

2 Put 15 g (½ oz) of butter to heat in another enamelled cast-iron casserole. Season the pieces of chicken on all sides with salt and pepper and put them in the casserole. Let them brown rapidly on all sides, and then place the pieces in the first casserole (1) on top of the bed of tomatoes and onions. Return the casserole to a gentle heat and cook, covered, watching carefully to see that the liquid does not all evaporate. The chicken should remain on top of the vegetables, cooking in the steam alone. After about 25 minutes, when the chicken is done, put the pieces on a plate and keep hot.

3 While the chicken is cooking, heat the 15 g (½ oz) butter in the casserole in which the chicken has browned and pour in the wine vinegar. Reduce until it forms a syrupy glaze and then add the red wine. Reduce again until there are approximately 5 table-spoons of liquid left. Remove from the heat.

4 Remove the bouquet garni from the vegetables in the first cas-serole (1) and liquidise the contents, or sieve them through a mouli-légumes. Pour the resulting purée into the second casserole contain-ing the wine and vinegar reduction (3). Bring to the boil briefly and strain the sauce through a fine wire sieve. Return to the cas-serole and add the pieces of chicken, which you have kept hot, together with the juices that will have run out of them. Allow to simmer for 5 minutes and then, away from the heat, add 15 g (½ oz) of butter swirling the sauce round in the pan. Finish by adding more salt and pepper if necessary. Serve the dish steaming in its casserole.

Fricassee of Chicken with Fresh Garden Herbs

Fricassée de volaille aux herbes vertes du jardin

For two people	Simple Inexpensive *Preparation time:* 20 minutes *Cooking time:* 35 minutes
Ingredients	1 white-fleshed chicken, of 1·5 kg (3¼ lb) 50 g (1¾ oz) butter 2 shallots 1 bunch of watercress 1 bunch chervil 1 bunch sorrel approximately 40 g (1½ oz) 200 g (7 oz) spinach 1 sprig tarragon 6 tablespoons whipping cream 1 egg yolk salt, pepper
Recommended wines	a mellow white wine such as Màcon, Burgundy, Pouilly fumé

1 Clean and singe the chicken, as if for roasting, and cut into four pieces – two with the wings and two with the legs. Make a small incision between the drumstick and the thigh of the chicken to speed the cooking process. Cut off the last joint of the wings.

2 Wash the herbs in several waters and drain carefully. Detach each leaf of chervil and watercress, and throw away the stalks. Do the same with the tarragon, but keep the stalks. Pull the green parts of the sorrel leaves away from the central stalk and roll them up like cigars. Cut each 'cigar' in fine slices to obtain thin ribbons called a chiffonade. Pick over the spinach and wash in several waters. Drain carefully, remove the stalks and make a chiffonade in the same way as for the sorrel. Peel the shallots and chop them.

3 Butter the bottom of an enamelled cast-iron casserole generously, with 30 g (1 oz) of butter. Strew it with chopped shallots. Salt and pepper each piece of chicken and place them on the bottom of the casserole. Add the tarragon, cover, and cook very gently over a very low heat for 25 minutes. The chicken should remain white and the butter should not have coloured. For this operation, known as cooking *à l'étuvée*, it is vital that the heat be very low and the lid of the casserole tightly fitting. When the chicken is done a knife point inserted in the thigh will produce a bead of colourless liquid. If the liquid is still rosy, continue the cooking for a few minutes more.

4 While the chicken is cooking, put 20 g ($\frac{3}{4}$ oz) butter to heat in a large saucepan over a fierce heat. Throw in the spinach (2) and stir with a wooden spatula until there is not a drop of water left. Add the rest of the herbs (chervil, sorrel, tarragon, watercress) and let them wilt over the heat, stirring with the spatula for 3–4 minutes. Put on one side, uncovered.

5 When the chicken is cooked remove it from the casserole and keep hot. Return the casserole to the stove, take out the tarragon stalk, turn up the heat, add 5 tablespoons of the cream and allow to boil for 3–4 minutes. Mix the remaining cream with the egg yolk in a bowl. Add the herbs and vegetables (4) to the casserole, bring almost to boiling point and remove from the heat. Pour in the egg/cream mixture and mix well. Allow the sauce to thicken a little over a very low heat. Season with salt and pepper. Arrange the pieces of chicken on hot plates and cover with the sauce. The garden has come to your table!

Little Quails in Baked Potatoes
Petites cailles en robe des champs

For two people   Fairly simple
Moderately expensive
Preparation time: 1 hour 30 minutes

Ingredients   2 wild or farm-bred quails (if in France ask for
the Princesse grade), plucked, cleaned and
trussed
2 large waxy potatoes weighing 250 g (8–9 oz)
each
60 g (2 oz) butter
1 tablespoon coriander seeds
salt, pepper

Recommended   Bordeaux (Saint-Emilion or Saint-Estèphe) or
wines   Coteaux d'Aix-en-Provence

1 Preheat the oven to 250°C/500°F/Mark 10. When it is hot put in the potatoes carefully washed but not peeled. They will take about 1 hour to cook, and can be tested to see if they are done by piercing them with a knife or skewer. If they are soft right through to the middle they are ready. If you have not managed to persuade your butcher to clean and truss the quails, do it while the potatoes are cooking.

2 Heat a frying-pan and toast the coriander seeds, stirring them about continuously, until they are uniformly done. Pour the seeds on to a cloth on a flat surface and, using a bottle, crush them to a fine powder, rolling them out as if you were making pastry. Using a fine wire sieve, sieve the powder on to a plate and set on one side.

3 15 minutes before the potatoes are due to be cooked, season the quails, inside and out, with salt and pepper. Put them in a small enamelled cast-iron cocotte just large enough to hold them, in which you have melted 10 g (½ oz) of butter. Brown them on all sides, then cover and cook for 15 minutes. Keep hot.

4 When the potatoes are cooked, take them out of the oven. Cut a 1 cm (¼ inch) slice off the long side of each potato and set these slices aside. Remove the cooked potato from each potato skin with a spoon without piercing the skin. Collect the potato in a bowl and, without letting it get cold, incorporate 50 g (1½ oz) butter cut into small pieces, and the coriander powder (2). Season with salt. Work the mixture to a smooth purée with a fork. Put a third of the purée in the bottoms of the two potato skins and put a roasted quail in each. Spoon the rest of the potato purée round and over the quails. Smooth the surface and put on the 'lids' – the slices which you have kept on one side. Put back in the hot oven for 5 minutes and serve in a folded napkin accompanied with a salad of lamb's lettuce (mâche) or other salad in season.

✱ As we say at Mougins, 'Té, vous m'en direz des nouvelles' ('*Now*, you're talking').

Vineyard Thrushes Cooked with Olives

Grives de vigne confites aux olives

For two people

Simple
Moderately expensive
Preparation time: 30 minutes
Cooking time: 4 hours

Ingredients

6 plucked thrushes, with their heads, which are, for true connoisseurs of this bird, the best part. Gut the birds or not according to taste. Personally I prefer not to
2 tablespoons olive oil
100 g (3½ oz) pork belly fat cut into little strips (lardons)
100 g (3½ oz) medium-sized black Niçoise olives
2 cloves of garlic
3 juniper berries
1 sprig of thyme
10 black peppercorns
1 tablespoon cognac
50 g (1¾ oz) flour
salt, pepper

Recommended wines

red wine such as Bandol, Coteaux d'Aix or a Côtes du Rhône

Editor's note

Since many countries outside France no longer see the charm in eating song-birds, it is encouraging to know that quails can be cooked in exactly the same way, with equally delicious results.

186

1 Stone the olives. Preheat the oven to 110°C/225°F/Mark ¼. Put the lardons and the olives in a small saucepan, and cover with 1 litre (1¾ pints) water. Bring to the boil and boil for 2 minutes, then refresh under a cold tap. Drain in a colander.

2 Crush the two cloves of garlic lightly and peel them. Season the thrushes with salt and pepper and arrange them in a terrine of a suitable size. Strew the olives and lardons (1) on the thrushes, then add the cloves of garlic, juniper berries, thyme, peppercorns, olive oil, cognac and 2 tablespoons water. Cover the terrine. Mix the flour with 4 tablespoons water in a bowl. Knead until you have a thick paste which sticks to the fingers. Seal the lid of the terrine in place with this paste and put it in the oven. Forget about it for 4 hours.

3 When the terrine is ready, take it to the table and remove the lid. Provence will greet you as you do so. Serve with a salad of curly endive and red radicchio trevisano, dressed with olive oil and wine vinegar.

✳ I'd like to tell you a story that will make the RSPCA tremble with rage and elicit cries of horror from all the old maids. My friend F (I won't mention his name as he would be arrested for poaching) is a peasant in the Var, and from time to time he traps little birds – robins, starlings, anything that catches his fancy. He plucks and roasts them. Then he cuts a pain-baguette in two lengthways and sprinkles it with olive oil. He lays the roasted birds carefully on the bread, pours the roasting juices over them, and puts the other half of the bread on top to make a sandwich, which he then ties up with thread. He keeps it in a cool place until the following morning, when, setting out for the chase, he puts it in his game bag. At lunchtime he halts under the shade of an oak tree, takes out his bottle of red wine and his sandwich, and cuts the thread. And, whatever tender feelings which you may have towards all small birds, you can't blame him for saying 'By God, this is good'.

Rabbit with Basil Sauce
Cul de lapereau à la crème de basilic

For two to *three people*	Fairly simple Reasonable *Preparation time:* 45 minutes

Ingredients

the hindquarters of a domestic rabbit (1–1·2 kg (2 lb 4 oz–2 lb 10 oz) comprising the saddle and the two hind legs
1 tablespoon chopped shallot
3 tablespoons dry white wine taken from the bottle you plan to drink with the meal
20 g ($\frac{3}{4}$ oz) butter
1 small sprig of thyme
1 teaspoon chopped fresh basil
1 teaspoon freshly-chopped parsley
5 tablespoons whipping cream
1 egg yolk
juice of $\frac{1}{2}$ lemon (optional)
salt, pepper

Recommended wines

white wine such as Côtes de Provence, Hermitage blanc, Mâcon blanc, or Pouilly-Fuissé

1 If you have a whole rabbit cut it in two just behind the ribs. Make one clean cut to avoid crushing and splintering the vertebrae. You can keep the front half of the rabbit for another dish, (for instance the Rabbit in Jelly, page 67). Cut halfway through between each vertebrae with the point of a knife. Remove the kidneys and the fatty parts. Season all over with salt and pepper.

2 Spread the butter over the bottom of an enamelled cast-iron casserole just large enough to take the piece of rabbit, and put it in with the thyme. Cover the cocotte and cook over a very low heat for 20 minutes. Check carefully every now and then to see that the rabbit does not start to brown. If the butter turns oily, add 2 tablespoons warm water and lower the heat. Keep the pan well covered. The rabbit is perfectly cooked when a fork inserted in the thickest part of the leg produces beads of colourless liquid: if the juice is still rosy, cook for a few minutes more. When the rabbit is cooked wrap it in foil and keep warm.

3 Raise the heat under the cocotte, add a tablespoon of chopped shallot and 3 tablespoons dry white wine, and reduce until there are about 2–3 tablespoons of liquid left. Add $2\frac{1}{2}$ tablespoons cream and bring to the boil again. Whisk together $2\frac{1}{2}$ tablespoons cream and the egg yolk in a bowl. Pour the contents of the bowl into the cocotte off the heat and return to the heat, whisking all the time. Bring almost to the boil and strain through a fine wire sieve into a small saucepan. Season with salt and pepper. Just before serving, add the chopped basil and parsley to the sauce and, if you prefer a sharper flavour, the juice of half a lemon. Check the seasoning. Put the rabbit (2) on a serving dish and cover lightly with the sauce. Buttered noodles (tagliatelle) go very well with this dish.

Salmis of Hen Pheasant with Endives

Poule faisane en salmis à la mousse d'endives

For two people	Could be difficult Moderately expensive *Preparation time:* 2 hours
Ingredients	1 hen pheasant of 1–1·3 kg (2 lb 4 oz–2 lb 14 oz) 2 tablespoons cognac 4 coarsely-chopped shallots 1 chicken stock cube 1 sprig thyme 3 juniper berries 6 tablespoons red wine of the kind you are serving with the dish $\frac{1}{2}$ teaspoon tomato purée 40 g (1$\frac{1}{2}$ oz) butter
Recommended wines	solid red wines such as Beaune, Volnay or Margaux

✸ To choose a tender young hen pheasant you need to know what to look for. The spurs on the feet should not be too pronounced. The beak and breastbone should be flexible. (These points go for all birds.) To make sure the pheasant is fresh, ruffle the feathers. They should be perfectly dry. If the base of the feathers is damp the bird has been shot in the rain and there is a risk that it will have an unpleasant taste of feather. This also applies to pheasants that have been frozen unplucked or kept in a cold store. (Here again, these remarks apply to all feathered game.) Finally, make sure that the eye is clear and not sunken.

✸ I specify a hen rather than a cock pheasant because they are generally more tender and have the most succulent flesh.

1 Preheat the oven to 250°C/500°F/Mark 10. Pluck, gut, singe and truss the pheasant, leaving in the heart, lungs and liver. Season the bird inside and out with salt and pepper and put the thyme and juniper berries inside together with the heart, lungs and liver of the bird.

2 Place the pheasant in a roasting dish and cover with 25 g (1 oz) butter. Put in the oven and roast for 20 minutes, basting two or three times with the butter, and cooking the bird for 5 minutes on one side, 5 minutes on the other and for 10 minutes on its back to make sure it is evenly cooked. Then remove the pheasant from the oven and put it to keep hot. Pour off the cooking butter and replace it with the wine. Bring to the boil on top of the stove to dissolve the cooking juices which have stuck to the bottom of the pan.

3 Cut the trussing strings off the pheasant. Remove the liver, lungs and heart and set them aside on a plate. Retrieve the juniper berries and thyme and add them to the red wine in the roasting-dish (2). Cut the pheasant into four pieces – two with wings and two with legs. The flesh should be faintly rosy. Remove all the bones except the main bones in legs and wings. Butter a small casserole lightly and put the four pieces of pheasant in it, skin side up. Grate some pepper over them, cover the casserole, and put them over a very, very low heat. Chop the bones and carcass of the pheasant coarsely and put them in a saucepan with a tablespoon of butter. Sauté over a medium heat and when the butter stops sizzling, add the chopped shallots and the tomato purée. Allow to brown. Flame with 2 table-spoons cognac, then pour in the wine from the roasting dish (2). Reduce until there is no more than 4 tablespoons of liquid at the bottom of the saucepan, and then pour in hot water up to the level of the top of the bones. Add the stock cube. Cook for 20 minutes over a moderate heat, then strain the sauce through a fine wire sieve into another saucepan. Reduce again until no more than about 2 coffee cups of liquid remain.
While the sauce is reducing chop the heart, lungs and liver finely on a chopping board to make a smooth paste. Add this to the boil-ing sauce. Boil again and then pour the sauce, which should be slightly thickened, through a fine wire sieve over the pieces of pheasant in the cocotte. Just before serving, bring the sauce briefly to the boil again and season lightly with salt and pepper. (For the accompanying endives, see the next page).

Endive Mousse
Compote d'endives à la crème

Ingredients 4 medium size heads of endive (witloof
chicory, *see* page 46)
40 g (1½ oz) butter
1 chicken stock cube
5 tablespoons whipping cream
salt

1 Remove any wilted outer leaves and trim the back of the endives.
Cut off the top 1 cm (½ inch) of the leaves. Wash and cut each in
two lengthwise. Heat 20 g (¾ oz) of the butter in a frying-pan, and
brown the endives on both sides. Arrange them in an enamelled
cast-iron casserole and add water to cover. Add 20 g (¾ oz) butter
and the stock cube and cook over a moderate heat for 25 minutes.

2 Remove the endives to a colander and drain well. Pack them
tightly into a shallow gratin dish and pour the cream over them.
Cook in the oven for 10–15 minutes, until the cream has all but disappeared. The stock cube should have been sufficient to season the
endives, but taste and add salt and pepper if necessary.

3 Arrange 4 half endives with the remaining cream beside each half
pheasant with its sauce.

✳ The bitterness of the endive, offset by the cream and the sauce
accompanying the pheasant, will give you the pleasure of a dish
which has the warmth of autumn foliage.

Lamb Stew with Garlic Croûtons
(*Estouffade de gigot d'agneau avec les tartines d'ail*)

Provençal Stuffed Vegetables
(*Les petits farcis de Provence*)

Mikado Salad (*Salade Mikado*)
Harlequin Omelette (*Omelette arlequin*)

Lemon Tart, Orange Cream, Oeufs à la Neige with Peach Leaves and Praline, Winter Fruit Salad in Wine. (*Croûte au citron, Crème renversée à l'orange, Oeufs à la neige aux feuilles de pêcher et aux pralines, Compote de fruits d'hiver au vieux Bourgogne*)

Vegetables

Choosing Vegetables

Asparagus is in season in June. In my opinion the purple variety is the best, then the green and lastly the white kind grown in sand. The slender green wild asparagus which you can find on the hills of Provence, especially in tracts which have been burnt over, is perhaps the best of all. Cooked in an omelette it makes a real banquet. Whichever kind you choose, asparagus should be crisp and fresh. If you choose the green variety, make sure that the heads are still tight and have not started to open.

Aubergines are best small and very firm, the tender mauve ones are preferable to the black ones.

Broccoli This delicious vegetable, so appreciated in Italy, Britain, Australia and the United States, is not well known in France, where it often tastes of immature cabbage. I prefer the Italian broccoli, which is much greener and is sold in bunches every part of which is edible.

Carrots The fresh green of the leaves shows that the carrots are fresh. Carrots should be a bright colour, without brown marks. Tiny new carrots are almost translucent. The carrots which you find in the shops in winter have generally been stored in either sand or in cold-storage and can be identified by the thread-like roots they develop. They have a stronger flavour than the new season carrots and are useful in soups and sauces.

Cabbages Whether green, white or red, they should look very fresh, with firm leaves and the cut stalk should be white. A stale cabbage has a disagreeable rotten smell.

Cauliflowers As with cabbages the severed stalk should be white. The 'flower' should be creamy-white without dark patches.

Courgettes The ultimate in perfection is to find those which still carry their large yellow flowers, and which can be cooked just as they are, flower and all, without peeling. Cook them until they are still slightly crisp and serve with no more than a sprinkling of olive oil or a nut of butter. If you can only find 'flowerless' courgettes, choose the smaller ones, with a lustrous appearance and, most important of all, firm flesh.

French beans (haricots verts) should be firm to the touch, brittle and without strings. The finest of the fine are the tiny beans the size of the tine of a fork, with their little white flowers still attached. Like the *rose de Malesherbe* the flowers only last a single morning, so don't let night fall before you invite your guests. These little beans deserve the most tender care: pinch off the two ends and plunge them immediately into a large pan of boiling salted water – 5 litres (9 pints) to 500 g (1lb 2 oz). On no account cover the pan, and watch while the beans cook, which should take only a few minutes. Take out a bean every now and then to see how they are doing and when they are still slightly crisp remove them from the pan with a slotted spoon and plunge immediately into iced water. Drain in a colander. French beans which are to be served in a salad can be seasoned with a little wine vinegar, a tablespoon of olive oil, a pinch of finely-chopped shallot and some sprigs of chervil. They can also be eaten cold with a generous tablespoon of double cream and the juice of a lemon. These tiny beans also make worthy companions for other fine ingredients, as you will see in the section of this book which deals with salads.

Garlic should be firm to the touch and without green sprouts. New season garlic is best because it is less pungent and more subtle. For preference, choose slightly purplish heads.

Mangetout peas should ideally only be bought if the flower is still attached. Once it has faded they tend to become somewhat stringy.

Onions The silver new season onions are the mildest, and the purplish kind are less strong in flavour than the yellow varieties. All onions should be firm, without green sprouts and with a dry, papery skin.

Peas As with French beans and mangetout peas, the presence of a flower is a guarantee of freshness. The pods should not be too swollen and should be a bright lustrous green. Try a pod before you decide whether to buy or not. The individual peas should be oval, small and pale green.

Sweet Peppers I prefer to choose, for salads, fairly large red peppers and the smaller green peppers which are more delicate. They should be plump, firm and crisp, with a lustrous skin.

Potatoes The most important thing is to choose the variety best suited to the dish you want to prepare. Desirée, which is a fairly new yellow-fleshed waxy variety, is excellent, and useful for almost everything except potato purée. King Edward is floury with a good flavour and splendid for potato purée.
In general potatoes should be firm and without sprouts.

Salad plants see pages 46–7.

Shallots New shallots which still have their leaves are the most delicate. The large mauve kinds are rather strong so look for the smaller grey variety. As with onions you should choose firm, unsprouted specimens.

Spinach should be crisp, smooth and dark green.

Swiss chard (**blettes**) The ribs should be white and the leaves lustrous. The severed stalks should be very white and not discoloured.

Tomatoes Choose the smallest ones for salad, the largest for concasséeing (dicing) and the long 'plum' tomatoes for sauce.

Turnips should be very white, crisp and smooth-skinned. If possible, buy them in bunches complete with their leaves, which should be very fresh.

All vegetables, not just French beans, should be treated with great respect. Although they are normally treated as mere accompaniments, it is a very great mistake and a sacrilege. Nothing is more delicate, fine and delicious or more marvellous than the pure fruits of the earth. They really suffer from being handled roughly – heat makes them wilt, cold deadens them. But treat them lovingly and they will pay you back many times over.

Provençal Stuffed Vegetables
Les petits farcis de Provence

In Provence stuffed vegetables are part of the repertoire in many families; they can be served hot, warm or cold. They are easily reheated. They can be served as a first course, a vegetable, a main dish or a garnish.

By arranging them in rows according to the vegetable, you can make them look extremely agreeable. Of course, it's also quite possible to make only one sort. The most usual are tomatoes, courgettes and onions. For the best results it is advisable to see that the different vegetables are all the same size. All the stuffed vegetables are both simple and inexpensive.

Stuffed Artichoke Hearts
Coeurs d'artichauts farcis

For two people, six if you are also serving other stuffed vegetables or using the artichokes as a garnish, for instance, for a roast joint or grilled veal
Preparation time: 1¼ hours
Cooking time: 15 minutes

Ingredients
6 artichokes, preferably the small purplish ones, weighing about 200 g (7 oz) each
300 g (10½ oz) leaf spinach
6 anchovy fillets preserved in olive oil
50 g (1¾ oz) diced cooked ham
4 tablespoons whipping cream
1 egg yolk
30 g (1 oz) butter
salt, pepper

Recommended wines
Young fresh red wines (Provence, Beaujolais, Bourgueil)

1 Bring 5 litres (9 pints) water to the boil with 4 tablespoons coarse salt. Meanwhile, wash the artichokes and remove the stalks. When the water comes to the boil, plunge in the artichokes and cook, uncovered, for 45 minutes. To avoid overcooking test them after 35 minutes and again after 40 by removing one of the inner leaves. If it comes away easily, they are cooked. Refresh in cold water and put to drain, upside-down so that the water can run out.

2 While the artichokes are cooking, wash and pick over the spinach, wash it thoroughly in several waters and drain in a colander. Put 20 g ($\frac{3}{4}$ oz) of the butter to melt in a medium-sized saucepan, and when it just starts to brown throw in the well-drained spinach. Stir over a brisk heat until all the liquid is evaporated, which takes about 10 minutes. Remove from the heat and leave it in the hot pan to keep warm. Preheat the oven to 180°C/350°F/Mark 4.

3 Put the cream and egg yolk into a bowl and whisk them together thoroughly. Put half the remaining butter in a small frying-pan and melt the anchovies in it (this will take about 2 minutes) crushing them lightly with a fork. Add them to the cream in the bowl and stir. Return the pan containing the spinach to the heat and pour in the contents of the bowl. Stir with a wooden spoon until the cream has bound the spinach. Take the pan off the heat, add the ham, cut into tiny dice, and season with salt and pepper.

4 Remove the leaves and chokes of the artichokes and arrange the hearts on a gratin dish buttered with the remaining butter. Pile the spinach mixture on to them, pressing it with a fork.

5 Bake in the oven for 10–15 minutes.

Stuffed Aubergines
Aubergines farcies

This recipe makes six, which can be served
with other stuffed vegetables or as a garnish
for a roast leg of lamb.
Preparation time: 40 minutes
Cooking time: 20 minutes

Ingredients

6 small round aubergines weighing 60 g (2 oz)
each, **or** 3 weighing 150 g (5¼ oz) each
100 g (3½ oz) large black olives
6 anchovy fillets preserved in olive oil
1 clove of garlic, chopped
1 pinch thyme
2 tablespoons olive oil
salt, pepper

*Special
equipment*

It is most important to use stainless steel, silver
or enamel implements whenever you are
dealing with aubergines as they have a strong
tendency to blacken when they come in contact with other metals.

1 Preheat the oven to 200°C/400°F/Mark 6. Pull off (do not use a knife) the green rosettes from the ends of the aubergines. If you have six small aubergines, cut a thin slice, lengthways, from each. Cut round the flesh with a small knife and scoop out the pieces with a teaspoon. Take great care not to pierce the skin, which should be about ½ cm (¼ inch) thick. If you have three larger aubergines, cut them in half, lengthways, and remove the flesh in the same way. Arrange the empty shells in an oven-dish, salt them on the inside and sprinkle with a tablespoon of olive oil. Spread the flesh of the aubergines on a second oven-dish.

2 Bake the empty skins for 15 minutes and the flesh for 30 minutes. Remove the dishes, but do not turn off the oven, which will be needed – at the same temperature – for the final cooking process.

3 While the aubergines are cooking, stone the olives and chop them finely. Put them in a large bowl.

4 Heat 1 tablespoon of olive oil in a small frying-pan. Add the anchovy fillets and crush them lightly with a fork. When you have a smooth purée, add it to the olives in the bowl.

5 When the flesh of the aubergine is cooked, crush it lightly with a fork and add to the bowl, together with the chopped garlic and thyme. Mix everything together well, season with salt and pepper if you think it necessary.

6 Pile the mixture into the aubergine shells, pressing it down with a fork, and heat through in a hot oven.

Stuffed Mushrooms
Champignons blancs farcis

I give the quantities for 6 mushrooms, but as
they aren't really a dish to serve on their own,
it is best to put them with other stuffed vegetables or as a garnish for a roast or with
drinks.
Preparation time: 20 minutes
Cooking time: 25 minutes

Ingredients
6 large cultivated mushrooms – about 250 g
(8¾ oz) in all
1 slice white bread
40 g (1½ oz) salt belly of pork without skin or
bone
1 clove of garlic, chopped
1 tablespoon chopped onion
1 tablespoon chopped parsley
3 tablespoons olive oil
salt, pepper

1 Trim the mushroom stalks and then remove them. Wash and drain stalks and caps and chop the stalk coarsely. Preheat the oven to 200°C/400°F/Mark 6.

2 Cut the belly of pork into strips the size of matchsticks and sauté them briskly for 3–4 minutes in a medium-sized frying-pan, without letting them get dry. Drain in a sieve and keep on one side.

3 Cut the crusts off the bread and cut it into tiny dice. Heat 1 tablespoon of oil in the frying-pan and fry the croûtons, stirring them round until they are golden. Drain them in a sieve and keep on one side with the strips of pork belly.

4 Cook the chopped onion in a tablespoon of olive oil in a small saucepan until golden, then add the chopped mushroom stalks and the garlic. Cook, stirring with a wooden spoon, until the juices which run out of the mushroom stalks have completely evaporated. Remove the pan from the heat and add the strips of pork, croûtons and parsley. Season with salt and pepper and mix well.
    Season the insides of the mushroom caps with salt and pepper and fill them with the stuffing.

5 Arrange the stuffed mushrooms on an oiled baking-sheet, sprinkle with the remaining olive oil and bake for 25 minutes. If they seem to be getting too brown, add 1 tablespoon of water to the baking tray.

Stuffed Cabbage
Chou vert farci

For six stuffed cabbage leaves which can be
   served with other stuffed vegetables, or as a
   garnish for pot-au-feu, roast pork or
   poached or braised shin of pork.
Preparation time: 40 minutes
Cooking time: 30 minutes

Ingredients

1 fairly loose-leafed cabbage weighing about
   1 kg (2¼ lb)
100 g (3½ oz) cooked ham **or** cold roast pork,
   cut into small dice
2 tablespoons carrots cut into tiny dice
1 tablespoon celeriac cut into tiny dice
1 tablespoon chopped onion
1 clove of garlic, chopped
20 g (¾ oz) butter
250 ml (scant half pint) stock made with a
   chicken stock cube
1 small sprig rosemary
salt, pepper

1 Bring 3 litres (5 pints) water to the boil with 3 tablespoons of coarse salt. With a small sharp knife, cut out the stalk and wash the cabbage, in two or three waters. Drain. Preheat the oven to 180°C/350°F/Mark 4.

2 When the water comes to the boil, plunge in the cabbage and let it cook for 5 minutes, then refresh under cold running water. Spread a clean tea-towel on the table. Remove the outer leaves of the cabbage and cut away the tough central ribs. When you have six handsome leaves, each the size of a small plate, lay them out on the cloth. If the leaves are too small, use two.

3 Melt the butter in a medium-sized saucepan. Add the diced carrots, celeriac and onion and allow to soften for 10 minutes, stirring occasionally with a wooden spatula. Add the diced ham or pork and the chopped garlic and cook for a further 5 minutes over a low heat.

4 Divide this mixture into six and put it onto the cabbage leaves. Roll them up tightly into balls.

5 Put the sprig of rosemary in a small roasting-tin and arrange the cabbage parcels, close together, on top. Pour in the chicken stock, which should come three-quarters of the way up the sides of the stuffed cabbage leaves. Cook in the oven for 30 minutes, basting every 10 minutes.

Stuffed Courgettes
Courgettes farcies

For two people For two people, that is, three stuffed courgettes each as a main dish or first course. The six courgettes can of course be served to a larger number of guests with other little stuffed vegetables.

Preparation time: 40 minutes
Cooking time: 35 minutes

Ingredients 6 plump round courgettes weighing 80 g (2¾ oz) each. (You can also use the long variety, in which case choose ones 4–5 cm (1½–2 inches) in diameter cut into 6 cm (2¼ inch) lengths, but the round kind is better, if possible.)
30 g (1 oz) cooked ham, diced
3 large white mushrooms
2 tablespoons chopped onion
3 freshly-chopped sage leaves
4 tablespoons olive oil
salt, pepper

Recommended wines Young fresh red wines (such as Provence, Beaujolais, Bourgueil)

1 Put 2 litres (3½ pints) water on to boil with 2 tablespoons coarse salt. While it comes to the boil trim off the courgette stalks and cut a ½ cm (⅕ inch) round from the stalk side and set it aside. Do not peel the courgettes. When the water boils, plunge in the courgettes and the rounds you have cut off them and boil for 10 minutes. Refresh under cold running water and drain in a sieve. Hollow out the flesh with a teaspoon, taking great care not to pierce the skin. Put the shells and the slices on one side and chop the scooped-out flesh coarsely.

2 Trim and wash the mushrooms thoroughly in cold running water and chop them coarsely. Chop the ham into small dice. Preheat the oven to 200°C/400°F/Mark 6.

3 Brown the chopped onion in 2 tablespoons of oil, using the pan in which you have cooked the courgettes. Stir with a wooden spoon or spatula. This should take 7–8 minutes. Then add the chopped mushrooms, the diced ham and the chopped sage. Stir for a further 5 minutes, then add the flesh of the courgettes. Season with salt, increase the heat and stir briskly until the liquid from the courgettes has evaporated. Take care that the mixture does not stick to the bottom of the pan and burn. Taste, and season with more salt and pepper.

4 Arrange the courgette shells (1) on a baking-sheet or roasting-tin just large enough to take them. They should be packed in fairly tightly. Then put the stuffing (3) into the shells with a teaspoon, pushing it well down. Cover the courgettes with their tops (1) and sprinkle with 2 tablespoons olive oil. Bake in the oven for 35 minutes, keeping an eye on them and if necessary adding 1–2 tablespoons of warm water to the pan.

✸ If you are using long rather than round courgettes the method is exactly the same.

Stuffed Onions
Oignons blancs farcis

For six stuffed onions, to be served with other little stuffed vegetables or as a garnish for roast pork or veal.

Cooking time: Method I – 1 hour, plus 20 minutes to preheat the oven

Method II – 40 minutes

Ingredients
6 fresh white onions weighing 100 g (3½ oz) each
5 tablespoons double cream
30 g (1 oz) grated gruyère cheese
1 egg yolk
1 slice white bread
20 g (¾ oz) butter
250 ml (scant half pint) stock made with 1 chicken stock cube
salt, pepper

Recommended wines
Young red wines (Provence, Beaujolais, Bourgueil)

✻ Although it takes a little longer, the first method is infinitely better. In both cases I have given flexible cooking times because some onions will take longer than others.

Precooking the onions: Method I
1 Preheat the oven to 200°C/400°F/Mark 6. When it is hot, roast the onions, wiped but otherwise just as they are, in their skins, for 1 hour. After 50 minutes test one of them with a skewer, plunging it right into the middle of the onion. If it meets no resistance they are done; otherwise cook for a little longer and test again. When they are cooked trim off the roots and remove the skins. Lower the oven setting to 180°C/350°F/Mark 4.

Precooking the onions: Method II
1 Peel the onions and trim off the roots. Put 2 litres of water in a large saucepan with 3 tablespoons of coarse salt and bring to the boil, plunge in the onions and cook for 40 minutes. After 30 minutes test one of them with a skewer, if it pierces the onion easily they are done, otherwise carry on cooking a little longer and test again. When they are cooked, remove from the pan and refresh under cold running water. Preheat the oven to 180°C/350°F/ Mark 4.

Stuffing and cooking the onions
2 After precooking the onions (which can be done in advance) cut the tops of each onion and remove the insides with a teaspoon until only 2 layers of flesh are left. You are left with just the shells. Take great care not to pierce the skin. Chop the flesh from the insides of the onions very finely and put in a bowl.

3 Add the cream, egg yolk and grated cheese to the chopped onion and mix well. Season with salt and pepper and pile into the onion shells. Butter a roasting-dish just large enough to hold them and arrange the onions in it. Cut the slice of bread into tiny dice and toast them in the oven or under the grill. Put them on top of the onions and finish with a nut of butter.

4 Pour a few spoonfuls of stock into the dish, to come half-way up the onions. Roast for 30 minutes. The cooking liquid will reduce to 2 or 3 spoonfuls, and should be sprinkled over the onions before you serve them.

Stuffed Potatoes

Pommes de terre farcies

For two people   For two people as a main dish, or for six stuffed potatoes to be served with other stuffed vegetables or as a garnish.
Preparation time: 30 minutes
Cooking time: 30 minutes

Ingredients   6 potatoes, evenly-shaped and weighing 80 g (2¾ oz) each
120 g (4½ oz) button mushrooms
1 teaspoon chopped shallot
1 egg yolk
4 tablespoons whipping cream
1 teaspoon freshly-chopped parsley
1 teaspoon chopped chives
40 g (1½ oz) butter
1 chicken stock cube
salt, pepper

Recommended wines   Young red wines (Provence, Beaujolais, Bourgueil)

1 Wash and dry the potatoes, then scoop out the insides with a special potato spoon, a melon-baller or a teaspoon with sharp edges. Leave the thinnest possible outer shell. Preheat the oven to 200°C/400°F/Mark 6.

2 Trim and wash the mushrooms and chop them finely. Melt the chopped shallot in a small pan in 15 g ($\frac{1}{2}$oz) butter for 2 minutes, stirring with a wooden spoon or spatula. Add the chopped mushrooms and cook, stirring until all the liquid has evaporated. Remove from the heat. Beat the egg yolk and cream together with a fork in a bowl and pour into the mushrooms in the pan, stirring them together well. Return the pan to the heat and stir until the mixture thickens. Away from the heat, add the chopped parsley and chives, season with salt and pepper and set on one side.

3 Dissolve the chicken stock cube in the quantity of water indicated on the packet. Butter a roasting-pan just large enough to hold the 6 potatoes, and arrange them in it. Pile the mushroom mixture into the potato 'shells', firming it well with a fork. Put a nut of butter on each potato and pour in enough stock to come half-way up the sides of the potatoes. Bake for 30 minutes, basting with the stock every 10 minutes. The liquid should have almost totally evaporated by the time the potatoes are cooked, but if you suspect it is drying up too quickly add a little more stock.

❋ If you can only find large potatoes, use 3 and trim them so that you have 6 regular shapes.

Stuffed Tomatoes

Tomates farcies

For two people	For two people as a main course or for six stuffed tomatoes to be served with other vegetables. *Preparation time:* 20 minutes *Cooking time:* 20 minutes
Ingredients	6 handsome round tomatoes weighing 80 g (2¾ oz) each 80 g (2¾ oz) meat left over from a beef stew or pot-au-feu **or** use sausage-meat. The latter will be moist enough, but the former will need 2 tablespoons of the liquid or sauce in which it has been cooked 2 tablespoons finely-chopped onion 2 tablespoons chopped parsley 1 small clove of garlic, chopped 2 tablespoons olive oil 2 slices white bread a pinch of thyme salt, pepper
Recommended wines	Young red wines (Provence, Beaujolais, Bourgueil)

✳ My mother often prepared a big dish of stuffed tomatoes, interspersed with potatoes scooped out and stuffed in the same way, which we carried down to the local baker to be cooked in his oven. I seem to remember that my mouth was already watering on the way to his shop. But if I remember rightly, I was never allowed to fetch the cooked dish. Common sense. I might easily have treated myself to a solitary picnic. I was, and still am, exceedingly fond of this dish. But if being excessively fond of food is a fault, it is hardly serious.

1 Wash the tomatoes and remove the stalks. Cut a 1 cm ($\frac{1}{2}$ inch) slice from the tops. Press the tomatoes gently to expel the seeds and excess moisture. Sprinkle them inside with salt and leave upside down to drain. Preheat the oven to 200°C/400°F/Mark 6.

Using meat from a stew
2 Cut the meat into small dice about the size of peas and put in a large bowl. Add 2 tablespoons of the liquid from the stew, the chopped onion, garlic and parsley and the thyme and mix thoroughly with a wooden spoon. Season with salt and pepper according to taste.

Using meat from a pot-au-feu
2 Follow the same method using 2 tablespoons of the stock in which the pot-au-feu has cooked.

Using sausage-meat
2 Heat 1 tablespoon olive oil in a frying-pan. When it begins to smoke, add the sausage-meat, breaking it up well with a fork to prevent it forming little lumps. After 3–4 minutes drain the sausage-meat in a sieve, then add to the onion, garlic, parsley and thyme in a bowl and mix everything together well.

3 Cut the bread into small dice and toast in a heavy frying-pan until golden.

4 Pile the stuffing (2) into the tomato shells (1), pressing it down well. Put the little grilled croûtons on top, and cover with the tomato 'lids'. Arrange the stuffed tomatoes in a roasting-tin just large enough to hold them, sprinkle with 2 tablespoons of olive oil and bake for 20 minutes.

✳ The tomatoes can be prepared in advance, but should not be cooked until the last moment.

Artichokes 'à la barigoule'

Petits artichaux violets à la barigoule

For two people Fairly simple
Cheap
Preparation time: 20 minutes
Cooking time: 20 minutes

Ingredients 8 small artichokes of the kind which appear early in the season in continental markets. They are purplish in colour and are generally sold in bunches, complete with their stalks and leaves. If the tips of the leaves are at all prickly, reject them; they will be second-growth side shoots and are too tough.
1 medium-sized onion
1 small carrot
4 cloves of garlic
1 sprig basil
$\frac{1}{2}$ bayleaf
1 sprig of thyme
1 tablespoon chopped parsley
1 lemon
3 tablespoons olive oil
6 tablespoons dry white wine
salt, pepper

Recommended wines Dry white or rosé wines

1 Peel the onion and slice it; cut the carrot into fine rounds. Peel the garlic, and keep 2 of the cloves on one side. Chop the other 2 together with the basil and parsley. Remove all but 4 cm (1½ inches) of the artichoke stalks and trim about 1 cm (½ inch) of the leaves with a serrated knife. Remove the outer two layers of leaves from the base and trim the base and stalk with a small knife. Rub each artichoke with half the lemon and plunge them in cold water into which you have squeezed the other half. Take out the artichokes one at a time and remove the leaves and choke (the prickly part inside) with a teaspoon, and replace in the bowl of water.

2 Heat the olive oil in an enamelled cast-iron or stainless-steel casserole and lightly brown the sliced onion and carrot. Arrange the prepared artichokes in the pan, add the two whole cloves of garlic, the half bayleaf and the thyme, and season with salt and pepper. Pour in the white wine and add water until the artichokes are barely covered. Cover the pan and cook for 15 minutes on a moderate heat, then turn up the heat and boil until the oil and wine are thoroughly amalgamated. The sauce should be syrupy and thick. Remove from the heat and season with salt and pepper. Add the chopped cloves of garlic, basil and parsley, mix well and serve.

✳ This dish re-heats very well, but you must remember not to add the parsley, basil and garlic until the last moment.

My Ratatouille

La ratatouille niçoise à ma façon

For four people Fairly simple
Fairly cheap
Preparation time: 1½ hours

Ingredients 500 g (1 lb 2 oz) aubergines (choose small, elon-
gated ones with firm flesh)
500 g (1 lb 2 oz) courgettes (choose small,
slender firm-fleshed ones)
200 g (7 oz) onions (preferably small fresh ones)
100 g (3½ oz) plump sweet peppers with thick
flesh
600 g (1 lb 5 oz) ripe tomatoes
1 pinch thyme
3 finely-chopped cloves of garlic
10 basil leaves, chopped
1 tablespoon chopped parsley
150 ml (¼ pint) olive oil
salt, pepper

Recommended Dry white or young rosé wines (Provence,
wines Coteaux de Nice)

1 Peel the aubergines. Half-peel the courgettes in stripes to give
a green and white zebra-like effect. Cut both vegetables lengthwise
into pieces as thick as your thumb and keep separate.

2 Bring 2 litres (3½ pints) water to the boil and plunge in the tomatoes having first removed the stalks. After 2–3 seconds remove them
and refresh under the cold tap. Peel them and cut them in half,
then press each half in your hand to remove the seeds and excess
moisture. Chop into large dice and set aside on a plate.

3 Peel the onions and slice them finely into rounds. Set aside.
Remove the stalks from the peppers and cut them in half vertically.
Remove the seeds and slice downwards into fine strips. Put on one
side with the sliced onions.

4 Once the forced labour of preparing the vegetables is over, they are ready to be cooked. Put 3 tablespoons of oil in each of 2 shallow sauté pans and when it begins to smoke put the onions and peppers in one and the tomatoes in the other. Season with salt and pepper and sprinkle the tomatoes with a pinch of thyme. Cook the tomatoes for only 2–3 minutes over a brisk heat, then transfer them to a plate and keep warm. Cook the onions and peppers gently over a low heat for 15–20 minutes, without letting them brown, then add to the tomatoes.

5 Put 5 tablespoons of oil in one of the pans and cook the aubergines for 7–8 minutes over a brisk heat, stirring frequently. Drain in a colander over a bowl and return the oil to the pan with 2 tablespoons of fresh oil. Heat and add the courgettes. Let them brown for 7–8 minutes, then add to the aubergines in the colander.

6 When you are ready to serve the ratatouille, mix all the cooked vegetables in a saucepan and stir well with a wooden spoon. Heat through, season with salt and pepper and at the last moment add the finely-chopped garlic, parsley and basil.

✷ This ratatouille is good with grilled or roasted meat and, cold, as a first course.

✷ Normally ratatouille is made by simmering the vegetables for 2–3 hours. My recipe conserves the texture and freshness of the ingredients.

Les Oeufs au Plat Niçois
An excellent recipe using ratatouille – Heat 5 tablespoons of ratatouille and line an oven-proof individual egg-dish with it. Make two hollows with the back of a spoon and slide a raw egg into each. Season with salt and pepper. Cook for 2 minutes over a brisk heat and for 2 minutes in the oven or under the grill. It is simply delicious.

Saffron Risotto
Le risotto au safran

For two people   Easy
Cheap
Preparation time: 40 minutes

Ingredients   100 g (3½ oz) Carolina rice (round-grain)
a pinch of saffron
150 g (5¼ oz) ripe tomatoes
1 tablespoon chopped onion
300 ml (½ pint) stock made with 2 chicken
   stock cubes
3 tablespoons dry white wine
60 g (2 oz) butter
3 tablespoons grated Parmesan
1 sprig thyme
salt, pepper

1 Cook the chopped onion in 20 g ($\frac{2}{3}$ oz) butter in an enamelled cast-iron casserole for 5 minutes, without letting it brown. Meanwhile, make the stock with 2 chicken stock cubes and 300 ml ($\frac{1}{2}$ pint) water.

2 Pour the rice onto the onions in the casserole and stir until the rice is shining and coated with the butter. Pour in the stock, add the sprig of thyme and simmer over a very low heat for 20 minutes, covered. When the rice is cooked allow it to rest for 5 minutes, off the heat, before removing the lid.

3 While the rice is cooking, bring 1 litre ($1\frac{3}{4}$ pints) water to the boil and plunge in the tomatoes, having first removed the stalks. After 1 minute remove them and refresh under the cold tap. Peel them, cut them in half and press each half in your hand to expel the seeds and excess moisture. Chop them finely, and add to the cooked rice.

4 Just before you want to serve the risotto, return the casserole to the heat and add the white wine and saffron, stirring with a wooden spoon. Simmer for 2 minutes, then add the remaining butter and the grated Parmesan. Mix well and season with salt and pepper. Serve the risotto, which should be creamy, in the casserole.

✱ This risotto can be eaten as a first course or as an accompaniment for a dish with plenty of sauce.

Potato Galette
Galette de pommes de terre

For two people Simple
Inexpensive
Preparation time: 30 minutes

Ingredients 1 potato weighing 250–300 g (8¾–10½ oz) or 2
potatoes making up the same weight
120 g (4¼ oz) butter
salt

*Special
equipment* 1 mandoline

Editor's note A food-processor will slice the potatoes quickly
and efficiently.

1 Peel the potato and slice it very finely (or alternatively cut it into fine julienne strips). Spread the slices on a tea-towel to dry and season with salt. Melt the butter in a small saucepan and keep hot. Scour the inside of a frying-pan 20 cm (8 inches) across with a cloth or kitchen paper and a handful of salt. Do not then wash the pan, but just wipe it out carefully. Pour two tablespoons of melted butter into the frying-pan, taking care not to include any of the white residue which will have accumulated at the bottom of the pan, and proceed according to whether you have slices or strips of potato.

For slices of potato
2 Arrange the slices in the pan, overlapping slightly like the scales of a fish and sprinkle with 2 more tablespoons of melted butter. Arrange a second layer of slices and finish with the remaining melted butter – still avoiding the white residue. Put the pan over a moderate heat and shake it with a circular movement to prevent the potatoes sticking. Press the potatoes down firmly with the back of a slotted spoon.

For julienne strips of potato
2 Squeeze the julienne strips in your hands to expel excess moisture and spread them in the frying-pan. Pour the rest of the melted butter evenly over them.

3 Cook the potatoes for 10 minutes over a moderate heat and then turn the galette over with a spatula or palette knife. Cook for a further 10 minutes.

4 Before serving, drain off the butter by tilting the pan, meanwhile keeping the galette in position with a spatula. Then slide it on to a hot plate and serve immediately.

✱ This galette goes well with all grills and roast meat.

✱ I have given two methods for the recipe, both equally quick and easy.

Potato Purée

Pommes purée

For two people Easy – but not quite as easy as you might
think
Inexpensive
Preparation time: 40 minutes

Ingredients 400 g (14 oz) potatoes. Do *not* use new
potatoes, they are not floury enough for
this recipe
75 g (2½) butter
100 ml milk (scant quarter pint)
salt

*Special
equipment* 1 mouli-légumes with a medium blade

1 Peel the potatoes and cut them into large chunks weighing 40–50 g (1½–1¾ oz) each. Wash the chunks in cold water and put them in a large saucepan. Cover with cold water, season with salt and put over a moderate heat. Bring to the boil and cook for 20 minutes. The potatoes are done when you can pierce them easily with a small knife. Don't overcook them as they will absorb too much water and disintegrate.

2 Shortly before the potatoes are cooked, warm the milk in a pan and keep on one side, with a lid to prevent a skin forming.

3 Place the mouli-légumes in the sink and pour the potatoes and their cooking water into it. When they have drained thoroughly, place the mouli-légumes over the saucepan in which they have cooked and purée them quickly. Return the pan to a *very low* heat. Add the butter and stir with a wooden spatula until you have a smooth purée. Stir in the milk (2) little by little until the purée is the right consistency. The amount of milk needed will depend on the quality of the potatoes.

✷ You may think that no one needs to be told how to make mashed potatoes, but in fact very few people know how to do it properly. Follow my recipe and you will see the difference. It is a dish which is often treated carelessly, but which does in fact need care and attention.

✷ You should pay special attention to the following points:

Don't peel the potatoes until just before you cook them, or they will go hard.
Start them in cold water and don't let them overcook and disintegrate.
Process them as soon as they are cooked or they will become glutinous.
Work them thoroughly with plenty of butter, to make them really smooth.
Add the milk gradually, so you don't make the purée too runny.
Serve the purée immediately. It neither keeps nor reheats well.

Baked Potatoes with Cheese and Herbs

Pommes cendrillon

For two people
Simple
Inexpensive
Preparation time: preheating the oven, 20 minutes
Cooking time: 45 minutes
Finishing the dish: 20 minutes

Ingredients
2 handsome potatoes weighing 250 g (8¾ oz) each (Don't use new potatoes)
30 g (1 oz) butter
3 tablespoons double cream
½ egg yolk
1 tablespoon grated Gruyère cheese
1 tablespoon freshly-chopped parsley
1 tablespoon freshly-chopped chives
salt
nutmeg

1 Preheat the oven to 200°C/400°F/Mark 6.

2 Wash the potatoes under the cold tap, without peeling them, and when the oven is hot cook them for 45 minutes. They are done when you can pierce them easily with a small knife. Remove them, but leave the oven on at the same temperature setting.

3 Make an incision lengthwise across each potato and remove a wedge 1 cm (½ inch) across. Scoop out the flesh of each potato with a tablespoon, taking care not to puncture the skin, and leaving a thin layer of flesh.

4 Mash the pulp in a soup plate with a fork, adding first the butter and then 2 tablespoons of the cream. Mix thoroughly and season with salt and a little grated nutmeg and stir in the herbs.

5 Pile the mixture into the potato shells. Mix the remaining tablespoon of cream, the half egg yolk and the grated cheese in a bowl and spread a tablespoon of this mixture over each stuffed potato.

6 Put the potatoes back in the oven for 5–10 minutes to glaze to a golden brown and serve immediately.

✱ These potatoes go well with all grills and roast meat.

✱ This recipe can be prepared a short time in advance, but you must carry out steps 3 and 4 as soon as the potatoes are taken out of the oven. Don't put the stuffed potatoes in the refrigerator, and leave the final coating with cream, egg yolk and cheese mixture until just before they go into the oven for the second time.

Courgettes Cooked with Tomatoes
Tian de courgettes et tomates

For two people	Simple
	Inexpensive (in season)
	Preparation time: 30 minutes
	Cooking time: 30 minutes

Ingredients

1 large onion weighing 150 g (5½ oz)
400 g (14 oz) ripe but firm tomatoes
300 g (10½ oz) slim dark green courgettes, firm to the touch
1 clove of garlic
4 tablespoons olive oil
½ teaspoon thyme
salt, pepper

Special equipment

1 oven or gratin dish about 20 cm (8 inches) across

1 Preheat the oven to 250°C/500°F/Mark 10. Peel the onion and slice it into fine rings. Soften in half the oil over a moderate heat, stirring with a wooden spatula. Do not allow the onion to brown.

2 Using a potato-peeler, remove alternate 1 cm ($\frac{1}{2}$ inch) strips of peel from the courgettes to give a striped effect. Slice the courgettes finely and keep on one side.

3 Remove the stalks from the tomatoes, slice them finely and keep on one side.

4 Rub the oven-dish vigorously with the peeled clove of garlic. Spread the cooked onion (1) over the bottom of the dish and season lightly with salt and pepper. Arrange alternating rows of green courgette and red tomato slices on the bed of onion and season with salt and pepper. Sprinkle with the thyme and the remaining 2 tablespoons of oil.

5 Cook, uncovered, for about 30 minutes, pressing the mixture down with the back of a slotted spoon from time to time. The vegetables should be well cooked and lightly browned.

✷ This is a marvellous dish which goes particularly well with roast lamb.

✷ You can add a sprinkling of grated cheese.

✷ A delicious variation is to make 'nests' in the finished dish with a small ladle and slide a very fresh egg into each. Let the eggs set in the heat of the cooked vegetables and finish with a few minutes in the oven. (But take care that the egg yolks don't dry up too much.)

✷ It is equally good eaten cold (but not chilled).

Fricassee of Vegetables
La fricassée du jardin de mon père

For four people   Fairly simple
Inexpensive
Preparation time: 30 minutes
Cooking time: 20–30 minutes according to
the freshness of the vegetables

Ingredients   150 g (5¼ oz) strips of salt belly of pork the size
of your little finger and without the skin
70 g (2½ oz) fresh butter
12 fresh new onions of the kind called cebettes
or grelots
4 small tender-leaved lettuces
2 bunches of tiny carrots with their leaves
(about 30 in all)
2 bunches of tiny turnips the same size as
the carrots. They should snap like a twig
when broken
1.5 kg (3 lb 5 oz) peas in their pods. If you
can, choose pods which still have their
tiny white flowers attached
Some tiny new potatoes, freshly dug

Recommended   red, white or rosé wines,
wines   young and fresh

Special   1 enamelled cast-iron casserole holding 3
equipment   litres (5¼ pints), with a lid

Preparing the vegetables
1 Remove the outer skin of the onions, remove the roots and cut
off the stalks at the point where the leaves start to turn green.
Wipe them carefully with a cloth but do not wash them.
Wash the lettuces carefully in cold water, keeping them whole.
Drain on a cloth.
Scrape the tiny carrots with a small knife, remove the leaves and
any little roots and wipe them. Neither wash nor cut them.
The tiny turnips must be handled with great care because they are
brittle.

Remove the leaves and rootlets and then peel very finely with a potato-peeler. Wipe the peeled turnips, but neither wash nor slice them. Shell the peas. Do not wash them and discard any overlarge peas. Rub off the skin of the new potatoes with your fingers under the cold tap then dry them with a cloth. Don't let them soak in the water.

Cooking the vegetables

2 Heat the strips of pork belly and 10 g ($\frac{1}{3}$ oz) of the butter in the casserole, turning them with a wooden spatula so that they are cooked (but not browned) evenly. 2–3 minutes should be enough. Throw in the carrots, turnips, potatoes, onions and peas and add 4 tablespoons of water and a teaspoon of salt. Lay the lettuces on top. Cover the casserole and cook over a moderate heat for 20–30 minutes. The dish is ready when the potatoes are done, and you can judge this by testing them with a small sharp knife. Finally, add the remaining 60 g (2 oz) butter, season with salt if necessary and serve immediately.

✻ I advise serving this fricassee as a course on its own, because any accompanying dish would drown the delicate flavours of the tender little vegetables.

✻ Obviously, this dish is best of all if you have your own vegetable garden and can pick the vegetables yourself in the early morning or in the cool of the evening. But it isn't wholly impossible for town dwellers who can shop early, and who may be lucky enough to find perfect young vegetables on market stalls.

Editor's note For cooks outside France this delicate fricassee is sadly almost impossible to make unless you have access to a vegetable patch. The baby turnips M. Vergé recommends are the long thin kind, not the globular variety which are most commonly found in shops.

Vegetables in Aspic

*Aspic de légumes frais avec son coulis
de poivrons doux*

For four people   Fairly complicated
Inexpensive
Preparation time: 3 hours (of which 2 hours
   are chilling time)

Ingredients   200 g (7 oz) carrots
200 g (7 oz) white turnips
100 g (3½ oz) French beans **or** shelled petits
   pois
2 artichokes weighing 200 g (7 oz) each
   preferably the small purple kind
200 g (7 oz) courgettes
200 g (7 oz) asparagus
1 sweet red pepper
1 fresh white onion weighing 150 g (5½ oz)
1 tomato weighing 100 g (3½ oz)
1 medium-sized clove of garlic
4 sprigs of basil
1 bouquet garni made up of a piece of
   celery, a sprig of thyme, half a bayleaf and
   4 sprigs of parsley, tied with a thread
750 ml (1¼ pints) aspic (made with aspic
   powder mixed to the strength
   recommended on the packet or, in France,
   bought ready-made from a charcuterie)
2 tablespoons olive oil
salt, pepper

Recommended   dry white wines – Coteaux de Provence,
wines   white Beaujolais, Saint-Véran

Preparing the vegetables
1 Wash the artichokes, having first cut off the stems.
Top and tail the French beans and remove any strings, or shell
the peas.
Peel the carrots, turnips, onion and garlic.
Scrape the asparagus.
Remove alternate strips of peel from the courgettes with a
potato-peeler to give a striped effect.

2 Stick two skewers into the red pepper and grill it or hold it in
a gas or wood-fire flame until the skin is completely blackened.
(If you only have an electric stove place it directly on the hot-plate.)
Cool the charred pepper under the cold tap and remove the skin,
which should come away easily when you rub it lightly with your
fingers. Cut it in half, rinse out the interior to remove all the seeds
and remove the stalk. Cut the two halves into broad strips.

3 Slice the onion and colour gently in the olive oil. Cut the
tomato in eight pieces and add to the onions together with the
strips of red pepper, the garlic and the bouquet garni. Season
with salt and cover with 3–4 tablespoons of water. Cover the
pan and bring to the boil. After 20–25 minutes remove the
bouquet garni and liquidise the contents of the pan in a food-
processor or pass them through the fine blade of a mouli-légumes.
Season with salt and pepper and pass through a fine sieve. Chill
in the refrigerator.

4 Bring 2–3 litres (3½–5¼ pints) of salted water to the boil and
plunge in the two artichokes. Cook them for about 45 minutes,
without a lid. They are perfectly cooked when you can easily
detach a leaf. Put them to drain, head down.

5 While the artichokes are cooking slice the carrots, courgettes
and turnips into 1 cm (½ inch) slices. Do not mix up the different vegetables. Put them in three separate small saucepans,
with enough cold water to just cover the slices, and a very large
pinch of salt and another of sugar. Cover the pans, and cook
until all the water has evaporated. This method ensures that the
vegetables retain all their juices. When they are cooked spread
each vegetable separately on a cloth placed on a baking-sheet.

6 Bring 2 litres (3½ pints) salted water to the boil and plunge in the French beans or peas. Cook until they are just tender, drain and refresh in cold water.

Arrange them on the cloth with the other vegetables (**5**).

Remove the leaves and chokes of the artichokes (**4**), slice the hearts finely and add to the other vegetables.

7 Bring 1 litre (1¾ pints) salted water to the boil and plunge in the asparagus. Cook them until they are still just on the firm side and then refresh under cold water. Add to the other vegetables.

You now have all the vegetables cooked and laid out on the tray in separate piles.

Making the aspic
8 Heat the aspic until it is just melted. Pour in two tablespoons into each of the four chilled bowls and run it round the insides of the bowls until they have a fine lining of glistening jelly.

9 Pour 3 tablespoons of aspic into a deep dish or soup plate and dip the asparagus spears in it until they are thoroughly soaked. Divide them into four equal bundles and place one in the middle of each bowl.

Follow the same process with the slices of artichoke hearts and courgettes, adding more aspic to the plate as necessary, and arrange them on either side of the asparagus in the bowls. Keep any surplus courgettes on one side.

10 Take thirty or so slices of carrot and the same of turnip and dip them in the aspic, then stick them in a ring around the sides of the bowl, about 1 cm (¼ inch) above the artichokes and courgettes putting a round of carrot then a round of turnip and so on. The jelly will make them stick together quite easily. Put the rest of the carrots, turnips and courgettes on top of the asparagus in the middle of each bowl. Finish by strewing the French beans or petits pois over the top.

11 Remove the stems from the basil and chop the leaves coarsely. Mix them with the remaining aspic, which should now be cold and still just liquid (definitely not set). Season with two or three twists of the peppermill and pour over the vegetables in the four bowls. Put the bowls in the refrigerator to chill.

12 Just before you are ready to serve the vegetable aspic, line a serving dish or four individual plates with a thin layer of the red pepper purée (3). Put the remaining purée in a sauceboat.
Dip each bowl for a bare minute into warm water to loosen the jelly (which should now be set) and then turn out on to the dish or plates. The vegetables make a beautiful mosaic of colours, glowing in their jelly.

✳ This dish takes a long time to prepare, but it can be made the day before.

✳ Served with a cold leg of lamb stuck with slivers of garlic, this makes a splendid summer dish and is also a good idea for a party.

Noodles with Pistou
Nouilles fraîches à la crème de pistou

For two people	Simple Inexpensive *Preparation time:* 25 minutes
Ingredients	300 g (10¼ oz) freshly made noodles (tagliatelle) or 250 g (8¾ oz) good-quality dried noodles 1 clove of garlic 15 fresh basil leaves 20 g (¾ oz) butter 2 tablespoons double cream 1 tablespoon olive oil 100 g (3½ oz) finely-grated Parmesan cheese salt, pepper
Recommended wines	white or rosé Côtes de Provence

1 Bring 2½ litres (4½ pints) of salted water, with 1 tablespoon of olive oil added to it, to the boil, throw in the noodles separately so that they do not stick together. Cook at a rolling boil for 8–10 minutes.

2 While the noodles are cooking, peel and crush the clove of garlic. Chop it and the basil leaves as finely as possible and set on one side.

3 When the noodles are cooked (they should still be slightly firm to the bite) drain them in a colander. Pour the double cream into the saucepan and return the drained noodles with the butter and the garlic and basil. Season with salt and pepper and toss with two forks, taking care not to crush or break the noodles. Serve at once with a bowl of grated Parmesan.

✳ If you do not have fresh basil, replace it with a generous tablespoon of chopped parsley. It won't be at all the same thing, but you will be able to enjoy the flavour of garlic.

Danny Kaye's Noodles
Les nouilles de mon ami Danny Kaye

For two people	Simple Inexpensive *Preparation time:* 15–20 minutes

Ingredients	250 g (8¾ oz) fresh noodles (tagliatelle) or
	    200 g (7 oz) good-quality dried noodles
	    made with egg pasta
	5 tablespoons olive oil
	juice of half a lemon
	2 heaped tablespoons of chopped parsley
	6 chopped basil leaves
	salt, pepper

Recommended wines	white or rosé, unassuming and young – Provence or Beaujolais

(continued on the next page)

1 Bring a generous litre (1¾ pints) of salted water to the boil with two tablespoons of olive oil added. Plunge in the fresh or dried noodles and cook until they are still just firm to the bite. The cooking time will vary according to the quality of the noodles, so test them from time to time.

While the noodles are cooking, put the remaining olive oil in a bowl with the lemon juice, parsley and basil. Drain the noodles in a colander and add them immediately to the oil and herbs in the bowl. Season with salt and pepper, toss with two forks as though you are mixing a salad and serve as soon as possible.

✱ This is only one of a number of dishes I have had the pleasure of eating (washed down with an excellent Californian wine – white Chenin) in Danny Kaye's beautiful and welcoming house in Beverly Hills. I'd like to take this opportunity of paying tribute to a man who is not just a marvellous actor and an enchanting companion but also a real friend to the children of the world. This many-talented man expresses his love of truth and beauty in his grand passion for cooking. He is a very accomplished chef, particularly in the matter of Chinese cooking in which he is certainly the equal of any of the great Chinese chefs. Being a perfectionist, he naturally makes his own noodles. His recipe for them is simple, delicious, but not exactly economical. Imagine using a kilo of flour, *three dozen* egg yolks and a trickle of olive oil!

Spinach Ramequins
Dariole d'épinards

For four people
to serve with a
roast

Simple
Inexpensive
Preparation time: 1 hour

Ingredients

2 eggs
8 tablespoons whipping cream
8 tablespoons milk
100 g (3½ oz) cooked spinach
30 g (1 oz) butter
salt, pepper, nutmeg

Special
equipment

4 small ramequins (individual soufflé dishes)
    made of oven-proof porcelain or glass

(continued on the next page)

1 Preheat the oven to 170°C/325°F/Mark 3. Cook the spinach if you have not already done so.

2 Break the eggs into a bowl and add the cream and milk. Season with salt and pepper and grate in a little nutmeg. Mix thoroughly.

3 Put 20 g (¾ oz) butter in a 20 cm (8 inch) frying-pan and when it begins to colour throw in the spinach. Stir with a fork for about 5 minutes over the heat. Then add the spinach to the egg mixture in the bowl, and mix well.

4 Butter the four ramequins, using either a pastry-brush or your finger, making sure they are evenly coated. Ladle the spinach mixture into the ramequins. Cover the bottom of a baking-tin with a sheet of paper in which you have made two slits in the shape of a cross, place the ramequins on it, and pour in enough hot water to come three-quarters of the way up the sides. Transfer carefully to the heated oven and cook for 25–30 minutes. To serve, turn the spinach moulds out onto a hot serving plate.

✸ The sheet of paper is necessary because it protects the bottom of the ramequins from direct contact with the heat, which might cause the spinach mixture to boil and form bubbles. The reason for the slits is to prevent the paper rising up like a balloon and upsetting the ramequins.

✸ You can add a tablespoon of currants, boiled briefly in 1 litre (1¾ pints) water and refreshed under cold water. Or again, a spoonful of flaked and lightly toasted almonds are an excellent addition.

Potato and Leek Ramequins
Dariole de pommes aux poireaux

For four people to serve with a roast	Simple Inexpensive *Preparation time:* 2 hours (including 15 minutes to preheat the oven)

Ingredients	1 potato weighing 200 g (7 oz) 1 potato weighing 150 g (5½ oz) 2 eggs 8 tablespoons whipping cream 8 tablespoons milk 1 leek weighing 75 g (2½ oz) 1 tablespoon butter salt, pepper, nutmeg

Special equipment	4 small ramequins (individual soufflé dishes) made of oven-proof porcelain or glass

(continued on the next page)

1 Preheat the oven to 200°C/400°F/Mark 6. Peel and wash the smaller of the two potatoes. Remove the outer skins and roots of the leek, cut it in half and wash it carefully, separating the layers to remove all traces of grit.

2 Bake the larger potato, washed but not peeled, in the oven for 40 minutes. Test it with the point of a small knife to make sure that it is cooked.

3 Cut the leek lengthwise into julienne strips and put in a small saucepan with half a tablespoon of the butter and 2 tablespoons of water. Cook over a moderate heat for 10 minutes until the water has completely evaporated. Remove from the heat and keep hot. Cut the small potato into dice and rinse under the cold tap in a colander. Leave to drain.

4 Warm through the milk and cream in a small saucepan and meanwhile beat the two eggs in a bowl.

5 When the large potato is cooked (2) lower the heat of the oven to 170°C/325°F/Mark 3. Cut the baked potato into four and scoop out the inside with a spoon. Sieve the flesh through a mouli-légumes into a large bowl and whisk in the warm milk and cream. Add the beaten eggs and whisk until all the ingredients are thoroughly mixed. Season with salt and pepper and 2–3 gratings of nutmeg. Add the cooked leek and the diced raw potato (3) and stir lightly to distribute them evenly.

6 Butter each ramequin, using a pastry-brush or your finger, and making sure that they are evenly coated. Ladle the mixture into the ramequins and place them in a pan of water prepared as de-scribed in the previous recipe. Cook in the oven for 25 minutes. To serve, simply turn out the potato and leek moulds on to a heated serving plate.

Cheese

Goat Cheeses Marinated in Oil with Herbs

Picodons marinés à l'huile d'herbes sèches

Simple
Moderately expensive
Preparation time: 10 minutes
Marination: 1 week minimum, 1 month maximum

Ingredients

6 picodon cheeses (goat cheeses from the Dauphiné, in season from September to December. If possible, choose farm-produced cheeses, not too fresh, with a fairly dry consistency.)
300 ml (⅔ pint) best olive oil
1 whole clove of garlic
1 handsome sprig dried thyme
1 handsome sprig dried rosemary
1 handsome sprig dried wild thyme (sarriette, known in Provence as pèbre d'aï – asses' pepper)
5 whole black peppercorns
5 coriander seeds

Special equipment

1 wide-mouthed glass preserving jar holding 1 litre (1¾ pints) with a hermetically fitting lid

Recommended wines

Hearty red wines (Côtes du Rhône, Coteaux d'Aix or red Bandol)

Preparation

1 Cut the cheeses in half across their width. Arrange the cheese and herbs in the preserving jar in alternate layers and sprinkle the pepper, coriander and garlic over the top. Pour in enough olive oil to cover.

2 Seal the jar and store in a cool place for at least a week and no longer than a month (if you leave it longer than that the oil turns rancid).

3 Serve the marinated cheeses with piping-hot slices of toasted French bread, sprinkled with the oil from the jar.

Fromage Blanc with Fresh Summer Fruits

Assiette de fromage blanc aux fruits frais du jardin

For four people Simple
Inexpensive
Preparation time: 20 minutes

Ingredients 4 pots (faisselles – see note below) fromage blanc, about 800 g (1¾ lb) in all
12 handsome strawberries
1 small Charentais or Ogen melon weighing 300–400 g (10½–14 oz)
2 pears
2 white-fleshed peaches
8 prunes from Agen or California
1 lemon
8 fresh apricots
12 fresh almonds
24 small lettuce leaves
8 fresh mint leaves
6 tablespoons whipping cream

Editor's note: Fromage blanc is traditionally made in France with curdled milk drained in little perforated metal or china moulds (faisselles). It can be bought commercially (but do not confuse it with cream cheese, which would be too rich for this dish) or you can make it yourself, in which case M. Vergé suggests you save the whey which runs out of the cheese to make a pleasant and refreshing drink. Curd cheese could be used as a substitute.

Preparation

1 Put the prunes to soak in a bowl of lukewarm water. Quarter the melon, remove the seeds and the skin and slice each quarter into four slices lengthways.

2 Plunge the peaches into boiling water for 2 minutes, refresh them immediately in cold water and remove the skins which will slip off quite easily. Slice into long thin slices. Cut the apricots in quarters.

3 Shell, skin and halve the almonds. Wash and hull the strawberries. Peel the pears, cut them in quarters and core them. Cut into fine slices and sprinkle with the juice of the lemon.

4 Pick over and wash the lettuce leaves without tearing them. Dry on a cloth.

Whew!

Serving

5 Take 4 large plates and place a portion of fromage blanc in the middle of each. Arrange six lettuce leaves round the edge, and on this leafy bed lay the various fruits, alternating the colours prettily. Crown the mound of fromage blanc with 2 mint leaves and 6 split almonds arranged like the rays of the sun.

6 Serve well chilled, with fresh single cream served in a jug, separately.

✱ This is a deliciously cool and delicate dish – ideal for summer lunch by the swimming-pool.

Fromage Blanc with Herbs
Fromage blanc aux herbes

For two people	Simple
	Cheap
	Preparation time: 15 minutes

Ingredients	2 pots (faisselles, see note on page 245) fromage blanc, about 400 g (14 oz) in all
	4 tablespoons double cream
	1 tablespoon wine vinegar
	2 tablespoons walnut oil
	1 tablespoon freshly-chopped parsley
	1 tablespoon freshly-chopped chervil
	1 teaspoon very finely-chopped shallot
	salt, pepper

Recommended wines	young light red wines (Beaujolais Village, red Sancerre, Côtes de Provence)

Preparation

Put all the ingredients into a large bowl, season with salt and pepper, and whisk thoroughly. Chill and serve just as it is in the bowl. If you have garlic growing in your kitchen garden add two or three of the tender inner leaves, roughly chopped.

✳ Ah! those summer evenings when my father set the dinner-table under the big lime tree. It didn't get dark till much later, but a peaceful silence had already descended on the Bourbonnais countryside. I was five years old, perhaps eight? even fifteen? It wouldn't have mattered, because my mother always looked the same as she carried out the big soup tureen of fresh milk from which she had skimmed a thick layer of cream. We always started the meal with large bowls of milk in which we crumbled pieces of pain de campagne, not less than a week old. We would go on adding pieces of bread until the last drop of milk had disappeared. Then, there was a bowl of fromage blanc prepared as I describe in this recipe, also brought up cold and fragrant from the cellar. With it we ate tiny new potatoes, cooked in their skins in salted water. That was our entire meal, but it brings back very pleasant memories.

Goat Cheese Croûtons with Thyme

Tartines de rigottes de Condrieu au thym

For two people	Simple Cheap *Preparation time:* 10 minutes

Ingredients	2 rigottes de Condrieu or Echalas (see note below) 8 thin slices of French bread 2 sprigs of dried thyme 4 tablespoons olive oil pepper

Recommended wines	Full-bodied red wines (Côtes du Rhône, Gigondas, Hermitage, Châteauneuf-du-Pape) or aperitifs

Preparation

1 Sprinkle the slices of bread with 2 tablespoons of the olive oil and brown them under the grill

2 Cut each rigotte into four slices horizontally, and place one on each slice of bread on the grill. Strew the leaves from the sprigs of thyme over the croûtons and add freshly ground pepper. Sprinkle with the remaining 2 tablespoons of oil.

Cooking and serving the croûtons

3 Just before they are to be eaten, grill the croûtons briefly for 3–4 minutes. The cheese will melt and turn a pretty golden colour. These croûtons can be served as a cheese course or with aperitifs before the meal.

Editor's note: Rigottes de Condrieu are small round flattish cheeses from the Lyons area. They were originally made only from goat's milk but cow's milk is now frequently added or used instead.

Roquefort Croûtons with Walnuts

Tartines de Roquefort aux noix

For four people	Simple Fairly cheap *Preparation time:* 25 minutes
Ingredients	200 g (7 oz) Roquefort cheese (ask for trimmings and crumbled pieces) 75 g (2½ oz) butter 100 g (3½ oz) shelled walnuts 2 tablespoons armagnac **or** cognac coarse country bread, three or four days old freshly-ground pepper
Recommended wines	full-bodied red wines (Cahors, Brouilly, Côte-Rôtie)

Preparation

1 Soften the butter in a large bowl, working it with a spatula. Chop the walnuts coarsely on a chopping-board, and mix them into the butter. Break up the cheese with a fork and add the crumbs to the bowl. Add the armagnac or cognac, give four or five turns of the pepper-mill and mix everything together with a spatula.

2 Just before you want to serve the croûtons, grill two good slices of bread and, while still hot, spread thickly with the cheese mixture.

✳ Well-blanched raw celery hearts and radishes go well with these croûtons. You can also try grapes, and peeled quarters of pear, first sprinkled with a little lemon juice to prevent them discolouring.

✳ In parts of central France croûtons like this, with a soup, make a meal on their own.

Puddings

Fresh Fruit Sorbets
Les sorbets de fruits frais

For two to three people

Fresh fruit sorbets make one of the very best of desserts, but they must always reveal the essential flavour of the fruit they are made of and be absolutely pure and natural. Made with nothing more complicated than sugar and the finest fresh fruit, they are inexpensive to make and extremely easy.

Obviously a sorbetière or ice-cream machine is essential if you want to be really successful. There are several small reasonably priced domestic machines on the market.

Most fruits lend themselves to the making of sorbets. I have given several examples in the following pages. Ideally, to disclose the true character and juiciness of the fruit, sorbets should be eaten soon after they are made

Equipment necessary for the making of sorbets

1 liquidiser, food-processor or mouli-légumes with a fine blade
1 fine nylon sieve or strainer
1 lemon squeezer
1 whisk

Editor's note As Roger Vergé says, it is very worth while investing in an electric ice-cream-making machine if you want to make really good sorbets and ice-creams, but the traditional method – freezing the mixture in the ice-making compartment of the refrigerator or in a freezer and stirring it occasionally with a fork as it crystallises – can be used if necessary.

Apricot Sorbet
Sorbet à l'abricot

Ingredients   300 g (10½ oz) very ripe apricots – preferably the very small 'muscat' apricots. You can use tinned apricots, in which case use their syrup instead of sugar
100 g (3½ oz) caster **or** icing sugar
1 lemon

1 Take out the stones and purée the apricots in a liquidiser or with the finest blade of a mouli-légumes. Add the juice of the lemon. Beat in the sugar with a wire whisk.

2 Transfer the mixture to the ice-cream maker and freeze it.

3 To serve the sorbet, scoop it into balls with a spoon dipped in hot water and pile it into well-chilled ice-cream dishes.

✳ You can break the apricot stones and take out the kernels, sticking them into the top of the sorbet before serving.

✳ If you have it, use icing sugar rather than caster sugar because it melts more rapidly.

Pineapple Sorbet

Sorbet à l'ananas

Ingredients   1 very ripe, fresh pineapple
100 g (3½ oz) caster sugar **or** icing sugar

1 Cut the top off the pineapple complete with its leaves. Put it into the refrigerator to chill. Hollow out the pineapple with a small knife, taking care not to pierce the outside shell which should be 1 cm (½ inch) thick. Put the shell in the ice-making compartment of the refrigerator.

2 Cut away the hard central core of the pineapple, and cut the remaining flesh into small pieces. Purée it in a liquidiser or through the fine blade of the mouli-légumes. Add 100 g (3½ oz) of caster sugar or icing sugar and beat it in with a wire whisk.

3 Transfer the mixture to the ice-cream maker and freeze it. Then using a spoon dipped into hot water, pack the mixture into the chilled shell of the pineapple. Put the tuft of leaves back on top, and serve.

Blackcurrant Water Ice

Sorbet au cassis

Ingredients   250 g (8¾ oz) fresh blackcurrants
80 g (3 oz) caster **or** icing sugar

1 Put aside two or three handsome bunches of currants (with leaves on, if there are any).

2 Remove the stalks from the rest of the currants and purée them in a liquidiser or with the finest blade of the mouli-légumes. Pass through a fine sieve, add the sugar, and beat it in well with a whisk. Transfer the mixture to the ice-cream maker and freeze. When you serve the sorbet scoop it out in balls with a spoon dipped into hot water.

3 Take the bunches of currants which you have kept aside and dip them first into iced water and then into caster sugar so that they are prettily frosted. Arrange them on top of the sorbets.

Lemon Sorbet

Sorbet au Citron

Ingredients   300 g (10½ oz) juicy lemons
5 large sugar lumps
100 g (3½ oz) caster **or** icing sugar
5 tablespoons water. Use a still mineral water to avoid the flavour of chlorine which characterises the water in some places.

1 Put 5 tablespoons of water into a bowl.

2 Wash the lemons carefully and then rub the skins with the lumps of sugar; the sweet-smelling oil in the skin will be absorbed into the sugar lumps. Put them together with the rest of the sugar into the bowl containing the water and allow to melt.

3 Cut the lemons in half and squeeze them. Pour the juice into the bowl through a fine sieve or strainer. Stir the mixture thoroughly. Transfer the mixture to the ice-cream maker and freeze. When you serve the sorbet scoop it out into balls with a spoon dipped in hot water and pile it into well-chilled ice-cream dishes.

Strawberry Sorbet
Sorbet à la fraise

Ingredients   250 g (8¾ oz) strawberries
½ lemon
80 g (3 oz) caster **or** icing sugar

1 Put two or three of the best strawberries on one side, complete with their green tops. Wash and hull the remaining strawberries, and purée them in a liquidiser or through the fine blade of a mouli-légumes. Add the sugar and the juice of half a lemon, and beat thoroughly with a wire whisk. Transfer the mixture to the ice-cream maker and freeze.

2 To serve the sorbet scoop it into balls with a spoon dipped in hot water and pile it into well-chilled ice-cream dishes.

3 Lightly moisten the whole strawberries which you have kept on one side, by dipping them into iced water and draining them well; then dip them into caster sugar so that they are prettily frosted. Place one on top of each sorbet.

Raspberry Sorbet
Sorbet à la framboise

Ingredients   250 g (8¾ oz) fresh raspberries
½ lemon
80 g (3 oz) caster **or** icing sugar

1 Purée the raw raspberries in the liquidiser or through the fine blade of a mouli-légumes, and strain the purée through a fine sieve or strainer. Add the sugar and the juice of half a lemon. Beat well with a wire whisk to dissolve the sugar. Transfer the mixture to the ice-cream maker, and freeze.

2 To serve the sorbet, scoop it into balls with a spoon dipped into hot water and pile it into well-chilled ice-cream dishes.

Melon Sorbet

Sorbet au Melon

Ingredients   1 Charentais melon weighing 500 g (1 lb 2 oz)
1 lemon
100 g (3½ oz) caster **or** icing sugar
a pinch of fine salt

1 Cut the melon in half horizontally. Take out the seeds and then scoop out the flesh with a tablespoon taking care not to spoil the green shells. Put these shells in the ice-making compartment of the refrigerator. Purée the melon flesh in a liquidiser or through the finest blade of the mouli-légumes, then strain it into a bowl through a fine sieve or strainer.

2 Add the lemon juice, sugar and a pinch of salt and beat thoroughly with a wire whisk to dissolve the sugar. Transfer to the ice-cream maker and freeze.

3 When it is ready scoop the sorbet into balls with a tablespoon dipped into hot water, and pile into the two green melon skins. You can crown each half with a strawberry.

Orange Sorbet
Sorbet à l'orange

Ingredients   400 g (14½ oz) juicy oranges
5 lumps of sugar
80 g (3 oz) caster **or** icing sugar
4 tablespoons still mineral water

1 Put 4 tablespoons of water in a bowl. Wash the oranges thoroughly and rub the lumps of sugar over the skins so that they imbibe the perfumed oil in the zest. Put the sugar lumps to melt in the water and add the caster or icing sugar. Cut the oranges in half and squeeze out the juice, straining it into the bowl through a sieve or strainer. Mix well with a whisk to dissolve the sugar. Transfer to the ice-cream maker and freeze.

2 To serve the sorbet scoop it into balls with a tablespoon dipped in hot water and pile into well-chilled ice-cream dishes.

William Pear Sorbet

Sorbet à la poire William

Ingredients   300 g (10½ oz) ripe (but on no account overripe)
William pears
2 lemons
80 g (3 oz) caster **or** icing sugar

1 Peel the pears, cut them into quarters and core them. Rub the pieces of pear all over with half a lemon to keep them white.

2 Put the quartered pears in a small saucepan with the sugar and just cover with cold water. Poach gently at a slow simmer for 10–15 minutes.

3 Take out the pears and reduce the cooking liquid by boiling until it starts to thicken and become syrupy, without letting it brown. Allow pears and syrup to get quite cold, then add the juice of a lemon. Purée everything together in the liquidiser or through the fine blade of the mouli-légumes. Transfer the mixture to the ice-cream maker and freeze. To serve, scoop the sorbet into balls with a table-spoon dipped in hot water and serve in well-chilled ice-cream dishes.

✳ In my opinion William pears have by far the best flavour and texture for the making of a pear sorbet.

Home-made Vanilla Ice-Cream
Les crèmes glacées

For two to three people	Simple Inexpensive *Preparation time:* 10 minutes *Freezing time:* 1 hour to 3 hours according to the equipment available
Ingredients	¼ litre (scant half pint) fresh full-cream milk 3 egg yolks 60 g (2 oz) vanilla sugar 2 tablespoons fresh double cream
Equipment	2 1 litre (1¾ pint) bowls 1 whisk 1 fine wire sieve

Put the egg yolks and vanilla sugar into a bowl and whisk for 5–6 minutes until light and creamy. Add the milk and 2 tablespoons of double cream. Whisk together. Strain into a second bowl through a fine wire sieve. Transfer the mixture to the ice-cream maker and freeze.

✳ Using this recipe as a base you can make several different ice-creams by adding, for instance, instant coffee or cocoa powder.

✳ This sort of ice-cream is not the same as those we make and serve in most restaurants, because of the extremely strict health regulations rightly imposed on us by the authorities. The only precaution you need take when making this particularly quick and delicious recipe is to eat the ice-cream the day it is made.

✳ To make your own vanilla sugar, you will need a 2 litre (3½ pint) preserving jar with an airtight lid. Put in 1 kg (2¼ lb) of caster sugar and 4 whole vanilla pods. Leave at least a week before using.

Anise Ice-Cream
Parfait glacé à la liqueur d'anis

For four to   Simple
five people   Inexpensive
Preparation time: 1 hour
Freezing time: about 6 hours

Ingredients   6 egg yolks
150 g (5½ oz) caster sugar
3 generous tablespoons Pastis **or**
   anise-flavoured liqueur
200 ml (⅓ pint) whipping cream, well-chilled

Equipment   1 saucepan large enough to act as a bain-marie
   for one of the bowls
1 skimmer
1 cylindrical or conical ice-cream mould (failing this, use a bowl)

1 Melt 125 g (4½ oz) of sugar with 5 or 6 tablespoons of water in a small saucepan and bring it to the boil. Remove this syrup from the heat, and keep it hot.

2 Put the egg yolks into one of the large bowls. Pour in the warm syrup and place the bowl over the bain-marie (the large saucepan of water). Bring the water slowly up to simmering point, whisking continuously so that the mixture thickens and becomes light and foamy. This takes about 7–8 minutes. Then take the bain-marie off the heat and continue to beat the mixture until it is completely cold.

3 Pour the chilled whipping cream into the second large bowl and whisk until it begins to thicken. Add 25 g (1 oz) sugar and continue whisking until the cream is thick and light. Whisk the egg mixture for a further 2–3 minutes so that it is at the same temperature as the cream. Then add the pastis or anise liqeur. With a spatula fold the egg-yolk and pastis mixture into the cream. When it is thoroughly blended transfer it to an ice-cream mould or bowl and put it into the ice-making compartment of the refrigerator. Allow to freeze for about 6 hours.

4 To serve the ice, dip the mould briefly into hot water and turn it out into a serving dish.

✴ The pastis can be replaced by any other alcohol or liqueur or even by strong coffee. The recipe is otherwise the same.

Prunes Steeped in Orange Pekoe Syrup with Cream

Pruneaux confits au thé de Lotus et à la crème fraîche

For two people	Simple Inexpensive *Preparation time:* soaking the prunes 12 hours finishing the dish 20 minutes
Ingredients	12 handsome Agen or California prunes 2 orange pekoe tea bags 150 g (5½ oz) caster sugar 50 g (1¾ oz) butter 250 ml (scant half pint) whipping cream 1 tablespoon icing sugar 2 tablespoons almonds cut in slivers
Equipment	1 large darning needle 1 deep dish 25–30 cm (10–12 in) in diameter
Recommended wines	a very cool sweet wine (Barsac, Sauternes)

Preparation: 12 hours ahead
1 Prick each prune with a darning needle, put them in a bowl, cover with lukewarm water and leave to soak for 2 hours.

2 Bring ¼ litre (scant half pint) of water to the boil in a small saucepan. Take it off the heat, drop in the teabags and leave them to infuse, covered, for 15 minutes. Then remove the teabags and add 150 g (5½ oz) of sugar. Bring to the boil, and boil for 15 minutes, skimming frequently to remove any scum that rises to the surface.

3 After the prunes have soaked for 2 hours and are nicely swollen drain them and leave them to steep in the tea-syrup for 8–10 hours.

Finishing and serving the dish
4 Put a deep dish into the ice-making compartment of the refrigerator to chill.

5 Soften 50 g (1¾ oz) of butter. Whisk the whipping cream to a light snow. Incorporate the softened butter. Add the tablespoon of icing sugar and chill for 10 minutes. Meanwhile toast the slivered almonds lightly to a pale beige colour.

6 Dip a tablespoon into a bowl of hot water and use it to make 12 nicely shaped balls of cream; place them in the chilled dish. *This must be done extremely fast.* Put a prune on top of each ball of cream and cover it lightly with a spoonful of the tea-syrup. Sprinkle the slivered almonds over the top and serve very cold.

Gratin of Oranges

Gratin d'orange

For four people	Simple Inexpensive *Preparation time:* 30 minutes *Finishing the dish:* 10 minutes
Ingredients	6 handsome oranges (choose seedless oranges if possible, but any will do, with the exception of Seville oranges, provided you remove the pips) 2 tablespoons whipping cream 3 egg yolks 6 tablespoons caster sugar
Equipment	1 saucepan large enough to serve as a bain-marie for the bowl 4 little fireproof cocottes
Recommended wines	Barsac, Sauternes, Vouvray

Preparation

1 Peel one orange very thinly with a potato peeler. Cut the ribbons of peel into tiny julienne strips either with scissors or a knife. Blanch this julienne for 2–3 minutes in a small saucepan containing 6–7 tablespoons boiling water. Drain in a sieve and refresh under cold running water for a minute. Put on one side.

2 Peel all the skin and pith from the other oranges leaving them completely nude. To do this use a very sharp knife, taking care to cut away every scrap of white pith and membrane as this gives the fruit a bitter taste. Divide the orange into segments, cutting against the fine inner membranes and holding the orange over a bowl as you do so, to catch the juice. Put the orange segments in a bowl, sprinkle them with 3 tablespoons of sugar and put them in a cool place.

3 Put the egg yolks, caster sugar, 4 tablespoons of orange juice and the tablespoons of whipping cream into a bowl and put the bowl over the bain-marie (saucepan of water). Put the pan over a low heat and whisk until the mixture becomes light and frothy.

4 Remove the bowl from the bain-marie and add the julienne of orange peel to the egg yolk and cream mixture. Divide the orange sections between four cocottes and spoon the egg yolk and orange mixture over the top.

5 Turn on the grill and let it get as hot as possible. Then put the dishes underneath to give the cream a light golden glaze. This should be done a few moments before serving.

✳ You can make a different pudding by replacing the oranges with raspberries or strawberries, and making the sabayon sauce with orange juice as before.

Tropical Fruit Soup

Soup de fruits des isles aux fleurs

For four people	Simple Rather expensive *Preparation time:* 1½ hours
Ingredients	2 pink bananas 300 g (10½ oz) fresh strawberries 12 lychees 2 ripe kiwis 4 slices fresh pineapple juice of 1 lemon 20 g (¾ oz) butter 1 tablespoon icing sugar 80 g (3 oz) lump sugar 300 ml (½ pint) whipping cream ½ teaspoon orange-flower water
Recommended wines	Sweet white wines: Sauternes, Barsac or Vouvray

✳ There are certain times of year when it is difficult to obtain, either in France or in the rest of Europe, the wherewithal to fill the fruit bowl properly, except with eternal oranges, tangerines, apples and pears. However it is at just this time that the markets suddenly offer a beautiful selection of exotically flavoured and coloured tropical fruits as fresh as if they had been picked the day before. I have invented this simple and unusual recipe to make use of all these different fruits.

1 Purée the bananas in the liquidiser or through the fine blade of the mouli-légumes. Mix this purée with juice of a lemon, 20 g ($\frac{3}{4}$ oz) of melted butter, and a generous tablespoon of icing sugar. Keep the purée in a warm place so that the butter doesn't congeal.

2 Put fifteen ice-cubes and a little cold water in the large bowl. Put the second bowl on top and pour in the whipping cream. Whisk with a wire whisk, incorporating the maximum amount of air, until the cream is firm but light. Quickly but delicately fold in the banana purée with a spatula. As soon as it is thoroughly mixed stop folding or the cream may turn into butter. Put this mousse in the refrigerator to set.

3 Dissolve 80 g (3 oz) of lump sugar in a small saucepan with 200 ml ($\frac{1}{3}$ pint) of water, and bring it to the boil. Add a few drops of orange-flower water and set aside to cool. Purée the 300 g ($10\frac{1}{2}$ oz) of strawberries in the liquidiser or through the fine blade of the mouli-légumes. Transfer this purée to a bowl and mix with the syrup perfumed with orange-flower water, making a thinnish purée. Chill.

4 Peel the lychees and the kiwis. Cut four slices of pineapple, removing the core.

5 Take a fairly large deep dish and pour in the strawberry purée. Dip a large spoon into hot water and use it to shape 4 large oval quenelle-shapes from the pink banana mousse. Arrange them in a star on top of the strawberry purée. Put three lychees on top of each 'quenelle'. Slice the kiwis into rounds and arrange them round the edge of the dish. Cut the slices of pineapple into lozenge shapes and stick them lightly into the 'quenelles'. Serve well chilled.

Bitter Chocolate Mousse

Mousse au chocolat amer

For four to five Easy
Inexpensive
Preparation time: 30 minutes – prepare at least
    1 hour in advance

Ingredients 125 g (4½ oz) bitter chocolate
15 g unsweetened cocoa powder
3 generous tablespoons very strong hot black
    coffee
60 g (2 oz) caster sugar
8 egg whites
pinch fine salt
½ lemon

Equipment 1 large saucepan to serve as a bain-marie for
    the bowls
1 2 litre (3½ pint) china bowl

Preparation

1 Put the bitter chocolate, broken into pieces, into a large bowl together with the hot black coffee and the unsweetened cocoa powder. Place the bowl over the saucepan of water and heat gently. When the chocolate has melted stir the mixture well until it is thoroughly blended. Take the bowl out of the bain-marie.

2 Clean the second bowl carefully, rubbing the interior with half a lemon. Rinse under cold water and dry carefully. Put in the egg whites which must on no account be chilled, add a pinch of salt and whisk until they start to form a light snow. At this point add the sugar and continue to whisk until the egg whites are dry and very firm.

3 Still using the whisk incorporate a quarter of the egg whites into the warm chocolate mixture. Now fold in the rest of the egg whites using a spatula, not the whisk, so that the egg whites do not fall. Transfer this mousse to a china bowl and place in the refrigerator for an hour to chill.

✶ This extremely light and only slightly sweetened mousse should ideally be eaten the day it is made.

Orange Cream
Crème renversée à l'orange

For four people

Simple
Inexpensive
Preparation time: 30 minutes
Cooking time: 40 minutes
Chilling time: 2 hours

Ingredients

½ litre (scant pint) milk
3 whole eggs
3 egg yolks
2 tablespoons orange liqueur
200 g (7 oz) caster sugar
½ vanilla pod
2 oranges, preferably seedless

Preparation

1 Preheat the oven to 180°C/350°F/Mark 4. Put 100 g (3½ oz) of caster sugar in a small saucepan with 2 tablespoons of water. Put the pan over a gentle heat and let the sugar caramelise to a good brown. Now add 3 more tablespoons of water, shaking the saucepan. Pour into the soufflé dish covering the bottom with a layer of caramel. Peel an orange 'à vif' – see page 265 for instructions – and slice into thin rounds. Arrange these on top of the sugar in the bottom of the soufflé dish. Put on one side.

2 Pour the milk into a saucepan and add 50 g (1¾ oz) of sugar and half a vanilla pod. Bring to simmering point over a low heat.

3 Put the eggs, egg yolks, 50 g (1¾ oz) of sugar and the finely grated rind of an orange into a bowl and whisk well. As the milk comes to the boil take out the vanilla pod, and pour the flavoured milk on to the egg mixture, whisking all the time. Strain through a fine sieve and add the orange liqueur. Pour the mixture into the soufflé dish lined with caramelised sugar and slices of orange.

4 Put the soufflé dish into the bain-marie (large casserole) with water half-way up its sides, and put the casserole into the preheated oven for 40 minutes. Make sure that the water in the bain-marie does not evaporate too much, adding more if necessary.

5 After 40 minutes take the dish out of the oven and allow to cool for at least 2 hours. To take the custard out of its mould slide the blade of a small knife all round the sides of the dish, then turn it over on to a plate, and give it a good shake. Serve at once.

Winter Fruit Salad in Wine
Compote de fruits d'hiver au vin

For two people Simple
Inexpensive
Preparation time: 1 hour. Make at least 2 hours
    in advance

Ingredients 2 passe-crassana pears (from Italy) **or** 6 small
    red cooking pears
8 dried prunes
1 orange
12 walnuts (24 halves)
1 bayleaf
1 small stick cinnamon
$\frac{1}{2}$ vanilla pod
1 clove
75 g ($2\frac{1}{2}$ oz) caster sugar
300 ml ($\frac{1}{2}$ bottle) full-bodied red wine (Côtes du
    Rhône or something similar)

Equipment 1 saucepan. A narrow deep pan is best so that
    the fruit is well covered by the wine

Preparation

1 Peel the pears, leaving the stalks on. Cut away the hard flower-part at the bottom, but leave them whole. Put the prunes to soak in a bowl of tepid water for 10 minutes. Open the walnut shells with a knife, so that you can take out the halves without breaking them. Cut an orange into $\frac{1}{2}$ cm ($\frac{1}{4}$ inch) slices, throwing away the two ends of the fruit.

2 Put the pears in a small deep saucepan with their stalks upwards. Drain the prunes and arrange them round the pears. Add the walnut halves, cinnamon stick, half vanilla pod, clove and bayleaf and caster sugar. Cover with the slices of orange and pour the wine over the top. If it isn't quite enough to cover the fruit, add a little cold water. Cook over a gentle heat for 30 minutes.

3 When the fruit is cooked leave it to cool for at least 2 hours. Before serving remove the cinnamon stick, vanilla pod, clove and bayleaf. Arrange the fruits in a small bowl. Pour the wine syrup over them and serve very cold but not chilled.

✳ This has a good 'hot' flavour for a winter's day.

Editor's note Unless your orange has a very thin skin you may find it better to peel it. In any case, the peel adds a bitterness to the syrup which may not appeal to everyone.

Chilled Fresh Figs with Raspberries

Figues fraîches rafraîchies aux framboises

For two people	Simple Inexpensive when figs are in season *Preparation time:* 20 minutes
Ingredients	6 fresh figs, ripe but not too soft, preferably 'muscat' figs 100 g (3½ oz) fresh raspberries 2 tablespoons redcurrant jelly 2 tablespoons eau-de-vie de framboise 3 tablespoons double cream 1 tablespoon caster **or** icing sugar 6 crystallised violets
Equipment	2 small iced plates
Recommended wines	Sweet dessert wines – Sauternes, Barsac, Vouvray

1 Peel six fresh figs (strip off their thin violet skins or just stroke them lightly with the blade of a small knife). Cut off the stalk. Make two cuts in the middle of the figs in the form of a cross, without cutting right through. Then, pressing lightly with your thumb in the middle of the fruit open out the four 'petals' of flesh. Keep them on one side. Put the raspberries into a bowl. Melt the redcurrant jelly and mix it while it is still warm with the raspberries. Keep on one side in a cool place.

2 Put the cream into a bowl together with the eau-de-vie de framboise and the sugar. Whisk until the cream becomes light and thick.

3 Cover the bottom of the chilled plates with this cream and arrange three opened figs on each one. Place a teaspoon of raspberries in the middle and crown each fig with a crystallised violet.

Bitter Chocolate Sauce
Sauce au chocolat amer

For five or six people	Simple Inexpensive *Preparation time:* 15 minutes

Ingredients	100 g (3½ oz) bitter chocolate 1 teaspoon caster sugar 2 tablespoons whipping cream 20 g (¾ oz) butter 6 tablespoons milk

Equipment	1 earthenware bowl 1 saucepan large enough to serve as a bain-marie for the bowl 1 medium saucepan

Put the chocolate in the bowl over a saucepan of water and put it to melt over a gentle heat. Bring the milk to the boil in the saucepan together with the whipping cream, 1 teaspoon of caster sugar and 20 g (¾ oz) butter. When the mixture comes to the boil add it to the melted bitter chocolate, mix it in well and then transfer to the saucepan and bring to the boil. Pour immediately back into an earthenware bowl and allow to cool away from the heat, whisking from time to time.

✱ To accompany vanilla and coffee ice-cream, iced coffee mousse, meringue glacée, pears poached in syrup with vanilla ice-cream.

Meringues

For 10–12 meringues

Inexpensive
Preparation time: 20 minutes
Cooking time: 2½ hours

Ingredients	5 egg whites
	375 g (13 oz) caster sugar
	1 dessertspoon melted butter
	½ lemon
	a little flour to dust the baking-sheet
	salt

Equipment	1 large bowl
	1 pastry bag with a 2 cm (1 in) nozzle
	1 pastry brush
	2 baking-sheets which must be spotless or covered with silicone baking-paper

Preparation

1 Preheat the oven to 110°C/225°F/Mark ¼. Melt a dessertspoon of butter and use it to brush the two baking-sheets. Sift a light shower of flour over the entire surface, shaking the tins lightly to remove excess flour. Using a round biscuit-cutter, or a cutter in any shape that you would like the meringues to be, mark out the baking-sheets by pressing it into the flour. This will help you to be accurate when you are piping out the meringue.

2 Clean the interior of a large mixing bowl with half a lemon. The lemon juice will remove any trace of grease from the surface, which might otherwise prevent the egg whites from rising properly. Rinse the bowl in cold water and dry it well. Put the egg-whites, without a trace of yolk in them, into the bowl. Whisk steadily, beating with an upward movement to incorporate as much air as possible with the egg whites. After 4 or 5 minutes, when they have started to rise, add half the sugar and continue whisking. When they have become very firm pour in the remaining sugar in a light shower, continuing to whisk.

3 When the whites have risen well and are firm transfer them immediately to the pastry bag. Pipe out the meringues on to the baking-sheets in the shape you have decided on. Put them into the low oven for 2½ hours. To help prevent them from becoming brown insert a third baking-sheet on the shelf above the meringues. When you take the meringues out of the oven allow them to cool and then put them in an airtight container, which should be kept in a warm, dry place. They will keep like this for several days.

✳ Serve plain, or stick two meringues together with Crème Chantilly or ice-cream and serve with bitter chocolate sauce, chocolate mousse, etc.

Light Iced Coffee Cream
Mousseux glacé au café

For four people	Simple
	Inexpensive
	Preparation time: 25 minutes
	Freezing time: at least 4 hours

Ingredients	700 ml (generous pint) whipping cream, chilled
	60 g (2 oz) icing sugar
	3 tablespoons instant coffee powder
	2 meringues made like flat curled snail-shells to the size of your soufflé dish
	4 round meringues (see recipe for meringues)

Equipment	1 soufflé dish 15 cm (8 in) across

Preparation

1 Put the coffee powder in the large bowl. Add a little whipping cream and beat well with a whisk. Pour in the remaining chilled cream and whisk until light. Sprinkle in the sugar in a fine shower, continuing to whisk until the cream is firm, but take care not to overdo it or it will turn into butter. Put in the refrigerator to chill.

2 Take the two flat discs of meringue, made by piping the meringue mixture in a spiral like a flat snail, and trim them so that they fit inside the soufflé dish. Keep the trimmings and cut the whole meringues into four or five pieces. Fold them with the broken pieces and trimmings into the coffee cream.

3 Put one of the meringue discs in the bottom of the soufflé dish. Fill the dish with the whipped cream and meringue mixture and cover with the second meringue disc.

4 Place in the freezer for at least 4 hours. Just before serving hold the base of the soufflé dish under the hot tap for a few seconds and turn out the coffee cream on to a serving dish. Serve with bitter chocolate sauce.

Melon and Redcurrant Cocktail

Cocktail de melon aux groseilles

For two people	Simple Inexpensive when currants are in season *Preparation time:* 30 minutes
Ingredients	2 small melons of 400 g (14¼ oz) each **or** 1 large one of 800 g (1¾ lb) 150 g (5½ oz) redcurrants 2 tablespoons caster sugar 5 tablespoons of Sauternes or Barsac – preferably the same wine as the one you are planning to serve.
Equipment	1 small spoon with rather a sharp edge **or** a melon-baller 1 bowl 2 small bowls
Suggested wines	Sweet dessert wines: Sauternes, Barsac or a sweet wine from the Roussillon

1 Cut the melons in half and remove the seeds. With a small sharp-edged spoon or melon-baller, carve the melon into small, even balls, putting them into a bowl. Scrape out the rest of the melon flesh with a tablespoon and share it out between the two small bowls.

2 Wash and drain the redcurrants. Keep back two nice little bunches, complete with their leaves if possible. Remove the stalks from the rest and put them into the bowl with the melon balls. Sprinkle with 5 tablespoons of Sauternes or Barsac and 2 tablespoons of caster sugar. Mix together well and then divide between the two bowls. Decorate each with a sprig of redcurrants – a perfect harmony of flavours and colours.

Sweet Flan Pastry
Pâte sablée

Simple
Inexpensive

Ingredients	500 g (1 lb 2 oz) plain flour 380 g (13½ oz) butter 150 g (5¼ oz) caster sugar 1 whole egg 2 egg yolks pinch salt 100 g (3½ oz) ground almonds the grated rind of a lemon 3 generous tablespoons dark rum
Equipment	Ideally use a food-processor or mixer. Otherwise you need a spacious work-top, your two hands and a certain amount of courage.

1 Mix together, either on the working surface or in a bowl, the flour, ground almonds, grated lemon rind, sugar and a pinch of salt. Cut the butter into large cubes and put into a well in the centre of the flour, together with the whole egg, egg yolks and rum.

2 Work everything together lightly until you have a homogeneous paste, *but do not overwork*. Collect the pastry up into a mass and cut it into 12 pieces of 100 g (3½ oz) each, rolling each lightly into a ball. Enclose each one in a plastic bag and keep in the refrigerator or freezer until needed.

✱ If you do happen to have a food-processor or mixer, proceed as before adding the ingredients in the same order, and putting the machine on at top speed. Stop as soon as you have a homogeneous paste.

✱ This recipe is given in a large enough quantity to make a dozen tarts for four people. The pastry is much easier to handle if it isn't freshly made. It can easily be rolled into balls of 100 g (3½ oz) each and placed in plastic bags. These will keep in the refrigerator for a week (take them out 20 minutes before rolling out), or in the freezer (take them out an hour before use).

280

Fresh Redcurrant Tart
Croûte aux groseilles fraîches

For four to six people	Simple
	Inexpensive
	Preparation time: 20 minutes (using ready-made pastry)
	Cooking time: 15 minutes
	Decorating the tart: 15 minutes

Ingredients	100 g (3½ oz) of pâte sablée (recipe page 280)
	600 g (1 lb 5½ oz) fresh redcurrants
	4 tablespoons redcurrant jelly
	a little flour for sprinkling over the pastry board

Equipment	1 pastry board
	1 rolling-pin
	1 baking-sheet

1 Preheat the oven to 200°C/400°F/Mark 6. Sprinkle the pastry board and the pastry with flour. Roll out the pastry into a round 25 cm (10 in) across. You will now have a flat disc of pastry without an edge. Place this round on a baking-sheet and prick it here and there with a fork. Put it in the refrigerator for 10 minutes, then bake in the preheated oven for 15 minutes. Allow to cool.

2 While the pastry is cooking detach the redcurrants from their stalks and put them into a bowl. Melt the redcurrant jelly in a small saucepan without allowing it to boil, then pour it over the currants. Mix it in well with a tablespoon, taking care not to crush the fruit. When the pastry is cool cover it with the currants and allow to rest for 15 to 20 minutes before serving.

Lemon Tart
Croûte au citron

For six people   Simple
Inexpensive
Preparation time: 20 minutes
Cooking time: 15 minutes
Finishing the dish: 5 minutes

Ingredients   100 g (3½ oz) pâte sablée (see page 280)
1 lemon
40 g (1½ oz) softened butter
2 eggs
80 g (3 oz) caster sugar
a little flour for sprinkling over the pastry
board

Equipment   1 pastry board
1 rolling-pin
1 medium saucepan, preferably not aluminium
1 wire whisk
1 lemon squeezer
1 baking-sheet

Preparation

1 Preheat the oven to 200°C/400°F/Mark 6. Sprinkle the pastry board and the pastry with flour. Roll out the pastry into a round about 25 cm (10 inches) across. You will now have a flat disc of pastry without an edge. Place this round on a baking-sheet and prick it here and there with a fork. Put it in the refrigerator for 10 minutes then bake in the preheated oven for 15 minutes. Allow to cool.

2 Meanwhile wash the lemon thoroughly and put the sugar, softened butter and eggs into the saucepan. Grate the rind into the pan, then squeeze the lemon and add the juice, stirring everything together thoroughly. Place the pan over a gentle heat whisking continuously, and bring the mixture slowly to just below boiling point. Remove the saucepan from the heat and dip the base into cold water to prevent the mixture from continuing to cook. Allow to cool.

3 When the pastry crust has cooled spread the slightly warm lemon mixture smoothly over the top with a spatula and allow to cool before serving.

Strawberry, Alpine Strawberry or Raspberry Tart
Croûte aux fraises de jardin, fraises des bois, ou framboises

For four to six people	Simple Inexpensive *Preparation time:* 20 minutes *Cooking time:* 15 minutes *Decorating the tart:* 15 minutes
Ingredients	100 g (3½ oz) pâte sablée (recipe page 280) 600 g (1 lb 5½ oz) strawberries, alpine strawberries or raspberries 4 tablespoons redcurrant or raspberry jelly flour for sprinkling the pastry board

1 Preheat the oven to 200°C/400°F/Mark 6. Sprinkle the pastry board and the pastry with flour. Roll out the pastry into a round 25 cm (10 in) across. You will now have a flat disc of pastry. Place this round on a baking-sheet and prick it here and there with a fork. Put it in the refrigerator for 10 minutes then bake in the oven for 15 minutes. Allow to cool.

2 Handle the fruit as little as possible particularly alpine strawberries and raspberries. Garden strawberries should be hulled, washed briefly in cold water and drained. Melt the redcurrant or raspberry jelly in a small saucepan, but do not let it boil.

3 Using a pastry brush, cover the cooled round of pastry with a thin layer of the jelly. Arrange the strawberries or raspberries on top one at a time, stalk ends downwards. If your strawberries are on the large side cut them in half downwards and arrange them cut side down. Brush the remaining melted jelly over the top of the fruit with the pastry brush. Allow to rest for 10 minutes before serving.

Walnut and Honey Tart

Croûte aux noix et au miel

For six people Simple
Inexpensive
Preparation time: 20 minutes (using ready-made pastry)
Cooking time: 15 minutes
Finishing the dish: 5 minutes

Ingredients 100 g (3½ oz) pâte sablée (page 280)
200 g (7 oz) walnut halves (preferably fresh)
5 tablespoons thick honey (preferably Provençal lavender honey)
6 lumps of sugar
3 tablespoons fresh double cream
a little flour for dusting the pastry board

Equipment 1 pastry board
1 rolling-pin
1 baking-sheet

1 Preheat the oven to 200°C/400°F/Mark 6. Sprinkle the pastry board and the pastry with flour. Roll the pastry into a round 25 cm (10 in) across. You will now have a flat disc of pastry. Place it on a baking-sheet and prick here and there with a fork. Put it in the refrigerator for 10 minutes then bake in the oven for 15 minutes. Allow to cool.

2 Meanwhile cut each half walnut into four pieces. Put the lumps of sugar in the saucepan with 4 tablespoons of cold water. Place over a medium heat and allow to caramelise to a light chestnut brown. Now tip in the walnuts and coat them with the caramel, stirring them about with the spatula so that they are well coated.

3 Away from the heat add the honey and cream, mixing them in well with the spatula until the mixture has cooled to lukewarm.

4 Spread the mixture in an even layer on the cooked pastry. Allow to rest for 20 minutes before serving.

Prune Tart with Armagnac

La tourte de pruneaux à l'Armagnac

For four people	Simple
	Inexpensive
	Preparation time: 20 minutes (using ready-made pastry)
	Cooking time: 25 minutes

Ingredients

100 g (3½ oz) pâte sablée (page 280)
250 g (8¾ oz) dried Agen or Californian prunes
5 tablespoons whipping cream
2 whole eggs
4 tablespoons vanilla sugar (see page 259)
3 tablespoons ground almonds
4 tablespoons Armagnac
2 tablespoons orange-flower water
30 g (1 oz) butter
a little flour for dusting the pastry board

Equipment

1 pastry board
1 rolling-pin
1 tart tin 20 cm (8 in) across

1 Preheat the oven to 200°C/400°F/Mark 6. Sprinkle the pastry board and the pastry with flour and roll the pastry out into a disc 25 cm (10 in) across. Lift it on to the tart tin and carefully line the tin. Prick the sides and bottom of the pastry with a fork and trim round the top of the tin with a small knife. Put in the refrigerator to chill.

2 Stone the prunes and put them to soak for 15 minutes in a bowl of warm water. Meanwhile put the whipping cream, eggs, vanilla sugar, ground almonds and orange-flower water in a large bowl and whisk them together. Melt the butter in a small pan and pour it into the batter, whisking it in thoroughly.

3 When the oven is ready, after about 15–20 minutes, take the chilled tart shell out of the refrigerator. Drain the prunes and dry them on a cloth or with kitchen paper. Arrange them on the bottom of the pastry and pour the batter over the top. Bake for 25 minutes. When it is done sprinkle the tart with 4 tablespoons of Armagnac and serve warm.

Tourment d'Amour

An Antillaise pastry

For four people   Simple
Inexpensive
Preparation time: 20 minutes (using ready-
    made pastry)
Cooking time: 25 minutes

Ingredients   100 g (3½ oz) pâte sablée (page 280)
6 tablespoons dried and grated coconut
8 tablespoons whipping cream
6 tablespoons dark rum or matured rum
3 eggs
6 tablespoons vanilla sugar (see page 259)
1 pinch ground cinnamon
a little flour for dusting the pastry board

Equipment   1 pastry board
1 rolling-pin
1 tart tin with a removable base 20 cm (8 in)
    across

1 Preheat the oven to 200°C/400°F/Mark 6. Sprinkle the pastry board and pastry with flour and roll out the pastry into a disc 25 cm (10 in) across. Lift it on to the tart tin and carefully line the tin. Prick the sides and bottom of the pastry with a fork and trim round the top of the tin with a small knife. Put in the refrigerator to chill.

2 Put the coconut, cream, eggs, vanilla sugar, pinch of cinnamon and 2 tablespoons of rum into a large bowl and whisk together thoroughly. When the oven is ready (after about 15–20 minutes), take the chilled tart out of the refrigerator and pour in the egg and cream mixture. Bake for 25 minutes. When it is cooked sprinkle with 4 tablespoons of rum and serve hot.

✷ There are two types of rum. Country rum which is a pure distillation of freshly pressed sugar-cane juice, and factory-made rum, which is made from molasses – which is in fact the residue left after the sugar has been extracted from the cane.

Both white rum, just as it comes from the distillery and brown rum are made in both cases. In the factory-made rum the brown colour is sometimes (possibly always?) achieved by adding brown sugar or caramel.

But the vintage 'country' rum is worthy of its name. It is aged in proper Limousin oak casks just like the ones used for storing Cognac and Armagnac; it is the tannin in the wood which gives the rum its deep colour. In fact, because of the climate and temperature, the rum usually stays in the cask for no longer than three or four years or its beautiful amber colour turns a greyish-brown. But even so there have been some old rums good enough to stand up against an excellent Armagnac. In matters of taste, assessing the merits of different alcohols requires the most educated palate.

Black Cherry Clafoutis
Clafoutis aux cerises noires

For four people   Simple
Inexpensive
Preparation time: 20 minutes (using ready-
   made pastry)
Cooking time: 25 minutes

Ingredients   100 g (3½ oz) pâte sablée (page 280)
300 g (10½ oz) black cherries
4 tablespoons whipping cream
2 whole eggs
20 g (¾ oz) butter
3 tablespoons vanilla sugar (see page 259)
3 tablespoons ground almonds
1 tablespoon Kirsch
a little flour for sprinkling the pastry board

Equipment   1 rolling-pin
1 tart tin with a removable base 20 cm (8 in)
   across
1 cherry-stoner

Preparation

1 Heat the oven to 200°C/400°F/Mark 6. Sprinkle the pastry board and the pastry with flour and roll the pastry out into a disc 25 cm (10 in) across. Lift it on to the tart tin and carefully line the tin. Prick the sides and bottom of the pastry with a fork then trim round the top of the tin with a small knife. Put in the refrigerator to chill.

2 Stone the cherries and put them into a small bowl. Put the eggs, cream, vanilla sugar, ground almonds and Kirsch into a large bowl and mix together thoroughly with a whisk. Melt the butter in a small pan and pour it into the batter, whisking it in well.

3 When the oven is ready, which will take 15–20 minutes, take the uncooked tart out of the refrigerator. Spread the cherries over the bottom and pour in the batter. Put straight into the oven and cook for 25 minutes. Take the tart carefully out of the tin and slide it on to a flat round plate. Serve warm.

Oeufs à la Neige with Peach Leaves and Pralines

Oeufs à la neige aux feuilles de pêcher et aux pralines

For four people	Fairly simple Inexpensive *Preparation time:* 1 hour
Ingredients	½ litre (scant pint) milk 5 eggs 6 fresh peach leaves 130 g (4½ oz) caster sugar 50 g (1¾ oz) praline (caramel coated almonds) 1 vanilla pod
Equipment	1 large, very clean bowl 1 smaller bowl 1 fine wire sieve 2 non-aluminium saucepans
Recommended wines	Sweet dessert wines: Barsac, Vouvray, Muscat

Preparation

1 Bring the milk to the boil in a saucepan together with the fresh peach leaves. Let it infuse for 5 minutes over a very gentle heat.

2 Meanwhile separate the eggs into two bowls (the one for the whites should be large and very clean) keeping the whites on one side, but not in the refrigerator. Add the sugar to the yolks and whisk well until light and pale. Pour the milk through the sieve on to the egg yolks whisking all the time.

3 Pour the mixture back into the saucepan and heat very gently, stirring with a wooden spoon until the custard starts to thicken. To tell when it is thick enough press your finger lightly on the back of the wooden spoon – if it leaves a trace in the coating of custard, it is ready. Pour the custard into a cold bowl and whisk it from time to time as it cools.

You must *never* let it come to the boil or it will start to curdle. If this happens whisk it energetically or put it into a bottle and give it a really good shake.

4 Put 2 litres of water, a vanilla pod and a pinch of salt into a fairly large saucepan and bring to the boil.

5 Beat the egg whites together with a pinch of salt. When they have become a soft snow add 30 g (1 oz) of sugar and continue beating to a very firm snow. Using a tablespoon, scoop the meringue into large balls. Turn down the heat under the saucepan of boiling water and put in the balls of meringue; allow them to poach gently for 5 minutes, turning them over half-way through the cooking. Then take them out carefully with a skimmer and put them to drain on a folded teatowel.

6 Pour the cold custard into a nice bowl and put the egg whites on top. Keep in a cool place. Crush the praline in a cloth with a rolling-pin or bottle. Just before serving sprinkle the praline over the egg whites and serve.

✳ Oeufs à la neige can be made 3 or 4 hours in advance, and the praline added at the last moment. If you can keep it in a cool larder this is preferable to a refrigerator. The peach leaves give the custard a light almond flavour, but can be replaced by a split vanilla pod or 3 tablespoons of very finely ground coffee (Turkish coffee) infused for 10 minutes in the milk in a covered pan.

✳ To whisk egg whites to their maximum volume it is important to follow some simple rules.

Neither the egg whites nor the bowl in which they are to be whisked should be cold.
The bowl and whisk must be spotlessly clean.
The whites must not have a single trace of egg yolk in them.
It helps to add a pinch of fine grained salt.
The best thing for whisking egg whites is still the good old balloon whisk; you can use a manual electric beater if you must, although in this case start slowly and gradually increase the speed.

Pink Grapefruit Grilled with Honey

Pamplemousse rose grillé au miel

For two people	Easy
	Inexpensive
	Preparation time: 20 minutes

Ingredients 4 tablespoons thick honey
2 pink grapefruit
Note: Make sure that the honey is good and thick – runny honey may melt before it has time to caramelise. When choosing grapefruit remember that the pink ones have more flavour and aroma.

Equipment 1 ovenproof dish
1 serving plate
1 very sharp kitchen knife
1 grapefruit knife
1 small chopping-board

1 Cut the grapefruit in half. Separate the segments from their membranes, using a grapefruit knife to cut round the outside. Spread a tablespoon of honey over each half grapefruit.

2 Heat the grill. When it is really hot, grill the grapefruit for 7–8 minutes. The heat will burst the top layer of their flesh and lightly caramelise it.

This recipe makes an unusual and delicious first course.

✳ Why not serve it with a generous slice of Parma ham?

✳ To help your grapefruit stand firmly cut a thin slice of peel horizontally from the base of each half.

Equipment

Editor's note

Roger Vergé's original list was slanted toward the kind of equipment used in a professional restaurant kitchen, including some types and sizes of utensil which the average cook at home would have neither space nor frequent use for. We have tried to simplify it, and at the same time add some of the useful gadgets called for in the recipes in this book. A home kitchen containing everything in the list would be very well equipped for almost every occasion, but as M. Vergé says at the beginning of the book, good cooks are always ingenious improvisers and remarkable results can be obtained with simple equipment. It is a good idea always to buy the best quality knives, pans and other metal utensils that you can afford, and a professional restaurant supply merchant is always worth a visit, especially if you expect to cook for large numbers of people.

2 large and 1 small wooden chopping-boards
1 large wood or marble pastry board 1 metre (40 inches) × 75 cm (36 inches)

A large heavy cleaver
Stainless-steel knives of various sizes including a serrated-edged knife, a long thin supple knife for filleting fish and small paring knives
A knife-sharpener or steel
2 potato-peelers
A semi-circular chopping knife and bowl
Kitchen tongs
A stainless-steel spatula
Cooking forks
Kitchen scissors
Skewers
A larding needle
A trussing needle and kitchen (non-nylon) string
An apple-corer
2 pastry brushes
4 wooden spatulas of different sizes, preferably in box or beech
4 bowl-scrapers

1 lemon-squeezer
A rolling-pin, preferably of boxwood
A nutmeg-grater
A grater for cheese and citrus peel
A mandoline
A large peppermill
A garlic press
An olive (or cherry)-stoner
A melon-baller
A tin-opener
A flour sifter
A corkscrew
Stainless-steel whisks of various sizes
A large balloon whisk
Ladles of various sizes including one with a pouring lip
2 slotted spoons
A fish-slice

Sauteuses (shallow saucepans) of various sizes according to your
    needs and storage space
Saucepans with lids, ditto
A fish-kettle with perforated grid
A steamer
A double boiler
A preserving pan
A ridged grill pan
Heavy frying-pans of various sizes
(If you cook on electricity or on a solid fuel stove, heavy reinforced
    pan bases are essential)
Enamelled cast-iron casseroles of various sizes, with lids
Enamelled cast-iron gratin dishes
2 pancake pans
Individual enamelled cast-iron egg dishes
Roasting-pans of various sizes including ones to serve as bains-
    marie
Wire roasting racks of various sizes
Rectangular aluminium baking-sheets
Cake racks
Cake tins
Flan tins

2 forcing bags with nozzles of various sizes
Fireproof porcelain soufflé dishes of various sizes
Fireproof porcelain individual soufflé dishes or ramequins
Rectangular terrines or pâte dishes in fireproof porcelain or metal
Preserving jars with airtight closures

Mixing bowls of various sizes made of stainless steel or earthenware
A pestle and mortar
2 colanders
A salad shaker
Conical metal and wire strainers
Sieves
Kitchen scales calibrated in metric and British measures
A measuring jug calibrated in metric and British measures
Meat and sugar thermometers
A food-processor *or* separate liquidising, chopping and mixing machines
A hand-held electric beater
An electric ice-cream maker (sorbetière)
A coffee-grinder